CONFIDENCE FOR TEENS UNLOCKED

EMPOWERING YOUTH TO FIT INTO THEIR
ENVIRONMENT, RELIEVE THEM FROM SOCIAL
PRESSURES OF LIFE, AND TO FEEL MORE
COMFORTABLE IN THEIR OWN SKIN!

DR. EMMA SKY

TABLE OF CONTENTS

INTRODUCTION

Have your parents ever rolled their eyes at you and told you that they were young once, too? I know; I feel for you. It's almost as if they think they can remember every detail of their perfect youth.

Being a teen today is actually quite a bit different from being a teenager 35 years ago. Back then, there was no internet or social media, and all your awkward moments faded into memory. I must say, I'm glad all my teenage blunders happened before the internet, and there was no online pressure when I was young. Most parents from this era won't entirely understand what you're dealing with.

The pressures teenagers face today are more real than ever. Life can be a whirlwind of challenges—that's not just your imagination. Social media is probably making you think that you have to be flawless, with followers constantly liking all your posts on social media. Then there's still good old school, exams, and wanting to make your parents proud. You may feel like you're supposed to have everything mapped out while you're still trying to juggle uncertainty and what comes next in your life.

Then there's life in general and all the doom and gloom that surrounds us. Your parents might also like to remind you how privileged you are and how tough life is for others, with all the global issues of wars, inequality, and natural disasters. This might leave you thinking, *why should I bother?*

Maybe you're struggling to fit into the mold of what's considered "normal" wherever you are. This, in itself, is exhausting. You might be making a huge effort, only to feel like you're just drifting further away from who you really are. This disconnect between your true self and the image you're trying to project to others could also be causing you more stress than you can imagine.

When you're stressed, it's not always easy to deal with life in healthy ways. Mental health challenges like anxiety and depression are affecting people at younger ages than ever before. If you're struggling, just know that you're not alone in this.

It might hit you as a wave of uncertainty or just the nagging feeling that something is off. The teenage years can be a wild ride for your brain, which is still forming and growing. Every experience you have during these years is shaping you in some way that you might not yet realize. You're not the only one still trying to figure things out. It's totally okay to look for guidance to get through this chaotic time, and that's also where this book aims to help you.

Self-help might sound corny to you at this stage, but the truth is that we all need a helping hand at some stage. We're all trying to make sense of things on this journey of life, and we're all looking for happiness.

Maybe you're wondering if you should give this book a shot. Well, absolutely, do it! There's nothing wrong with looking for guidance and support. You need to take control of your life and give yourself the tools to tackle your future.

Let's step into this journey of self-discovery together. This book could be just what you need to kickstart your journey to well-being and those successful first steps into adulthood. We're here to guide you and will walk next to you all the way. Throughout the book, some fun and engaging activities will help you grasp and experience the concepts even better. Let's jump in and enjoy the ride!

1

GETTING TO KNOW THE SELFIES

Ben was a talented athlete with a passion for basketball. He dreamed of making it onto his school's varsity team, but he felt a lot of self-doubt when he compared himself to other players.

Ben started believing he wasn't good enough, and his confidence was dented when he faced setbacks during the tryouts.

The mistakes he made on the court, such as missed shots, made him feel like he was losing and would never make it onto the team. Ben thought about giving up on his dream as he watched the other players move effortlessly on the court. They all seemed so much better than him and more confident. He thought they had it all figured out.

The next day, Ben's coach called him over and told him a story from his own high school days. It turned out that back when the coach was in high school, he also felt self-doubt and like he didn't measure up a lot of the time.

The coach assured Ben that setbacks didn't define his worth or his potential to succeed. He should only focus on his progress and not compare himself to anyone else. Everyone faced challenges at some stage, and it was just a part of becoming good at something.

The coach's words inspired Ben to embrace his uniqueness. He realized he had to work on his own strengths and potential and that he didn't have to be a carbon copy of the other players.

Ben started to view missed shots and other mistakes as opportunities to learn and improve. He committed to extra practice and worked on improving his skills. Ben realized that the journey to success would be a series of ups and downs and not a straight and easy path. He would have to work hard and not give up when he faced setbacks.

As time passed, Ben's strength and resilience became evident. His teammates and coaches started to notice his changed behavior and they respected his determination.

One day, during an especially intense game, Ben found himself facing a critical moment when a game's score was tied, and the pressure was mounting. Instead of losing confidence, Ben trusted his abilities. He used a bold move he had been working on; the ball flew through the net, and the crowd cheered. Ben felt proud of himself and like he had achieved something significant.

Ben became an inspiration to the other teenagers at his school. They learned that they should be passionate, resilient, and dedicated when pursuing their dreams, even when facing challenges and setbacks.

WHAT IS SELF-ESTEEM, SELF-CONFIDENCE, SELF-LOVE, AND SELF-RESPECT?

You've probably heard people talk about self-esteem, self-confidence, self-love, and self-respect, but do you know what these words mean? Maybe they were discussed in a class at school, and you weren't really listening because you didn't find the topic interesting at the time.

However, knowing the meaning of these terms can help you when it comes to your personal growth journey, which will involve building your own identity.

Self-Esteem

Self-esteem is how you feel about yourself and believe in your good qualities and abilities. If you recognize your worth, you'll value yourself as a person, and you'll feel good about who you are.

For example, Julia loved playing the guitar, but she always compared herself to others she thought were more talented and doubted her skills. One day, she gathered the courage to play for her family and friends. They applauded her efforts and she felt a sense of accomplishment. This experience boosted her self-esteem and she began to believe in her abilities. Her growing self-esteem encouraged her to further improve her musical talents.

Journal Prompts

Did you know that you can learn a lot by writing about yourself? We will ask you a few short questions after every section that you can answer in any way you want. You don't have to rush through them, and you only have to do one a day. It's all up to you. You don't even have to write your answers down; you can draw or make notes on your phone or tablet. You could even just think about the questions and how you would answer them.

Well then, let's get started with the first set of 10 questions.

1. Think about what you're passionate about, and also consider the reasons why.
2. Are there things you've wanted to express but you've been scared to do so?
3. Why are you afraid to express certain things? Are you scared of being judged and rejected by others?
4. Do you do certain things that make you feel creative and playful?
5. Do you express your creativity around others, or do you also fear judgment?
6. Do you do things to challenge yourself mentally?
7. How many things do you do daily to challenge yourself mentally and physically?
8. What challenging tasks have you accomplished? Are you always looking for new challenges?
9. How do you feel after you accomplish something?
10. Do you feel proud of what you have accomplished?

Self-Confidence

Self-confidence is about believing in your skills and talents and feeling capable of handling whatever happens in your life, including challenges and setbacks. If you don't have a lot of self-confidence at the moment, you can always get more by working on a positive relationship with yourself.

Celebrate your accomplishments, even if they don't seem that big to you. You could keep a progress journal and regularly read through it to remind yourself what you've achieved. If you make some mistakes and things go wrong along the way (as they tend to do), just remind yourself that you're always learning and improving. Setbacks are really just opportunities to learn as much as possible, maybe even faster than you would have learned otherwise. Remember that the only people who never make mistakes are the ones who usually don't do much in life.

You could also boost your self-confidence just by being kind to yourself. Treat yourself like you treat your really good friends who you want to keep around for the long term.

Self-confidence is something you can learn and improve over time, so believe in yourself and keep working to achieve your goals!

Journal Prompts

Ask yourself the following questions:

1. Will I do what my friends are doing, even though I don't really want to?
2. If I have different ideas from my friends, will I tell them?
3. What do my friends talk about?
4. Do I feel good when I'm around my friends?
5. What type of friends would make me feel confident?
6. How can I be more confident when I'm around my friends?
7. Do I believe I can be successful at school and accomplish what I want to achieve?
8. What amazing things does my body allow me to do, e.g., running, dancing, and eating?
9. Does my mind allow me to do amazing things? Does it allow me to be creative and succeed at school?
10. What things do I do to help me feel more confident about myself?

Self-Love

Self-love is about valuing yourself, caring for yourself, and treating yourself with kindness and acceptance, like you would treat your close friends. Self-love also means taking care of your emotional, mental, and physical well-being.

For example, Julia struggled with her appearance and compared herself to the other girls when she felt insecure.

Once she gained more self-confidence, Julia realized there were things she appreciated about her body. She made more time for self-care and treated her body more kindly to celebrate its unique qualities.

Journal Prompts

1. Write about a time when you were proud of yourself. What did you do, and what happened?
2. Think about the challenges you faced in your life. How did it make you stronger as a person?
3. List about five to ten qualities that you think make you unique as a person.
4. Think about how you can work on your self-love every day. Write down about five activities that you can do to help you with this.
5. Write down five things that you're proud of accomplishing.
6. What activities are you really good at doing?
7. Write down ten simple things that make you happy.

8. Why do you deserve to be happy?
9. Write down five things that you love about your body.
10. What do you like most about yourself?

Self-Respect

If you respect yourself, you treat yourself with dignity and honor yourself. You set boundaries in your relationships with others and make sure that they also treat you with respect. The life choices of people who respect themselves will also align with their values.

For example, Julia sometimes felt pressured by her friends to take part in activities she considered risky, such as drinking too much alcohol. She wanted to fit in, but she knew that these actions were against her personal values and that the outcome could be negative.

Becoming more confident and developing self-love helped her to set boundaries and stand up for her well-being. She declined invitations to parties where she knew there would be alcohol and drugs and focused on her studies and creative activities instead.

The world can be a confusing place, especially if you're feeling unsure of who you really are. You might be seeing images in the media and on social media of who you should be, or you could be comparing yourself to posts and photos you see on social media. Your parents, friends, and even religion could be telling you that you should behave in certain ways if you want to be accepted and respected. However, changing your identity to please others will just cause you to lead an inauthentic life and lead to unhappiness in the long term.

Journal Prompts

1. What does self-respect mean to you?
2. What brings you joy in life? Do you regularly do things that make you happy?
3. What makes you angry, and how do you deal with these things?
4. What is important to you in your life? Try to think of about five to ten things.
5. When you hear the word "values," what do you think about?
6. Think about someone you admire. How can you include some of their values in your own life?
7. Write a letter to your future self that speaks about the importance of self-respect and how important it is for your overall well-being. What actions can you take to improve your self-respect over time?
8. Do you have any critical or negative thoughts about yourself? How do these thoughts affect

your self-respect, and what can you do to deal with them?

9. Have you ever felt pressured by your friends to do something that goes against your values? How can you build the confidence to say "no" and stand firm in your decisions?

10. What successes have you experienced recently? In which ways do you celebrate your success?

Self-Discipline

If you have self-discipline, you can think about it as having your very own superpower. You're in control of yourself, you're able to make the best choices, and you can stay focused on your goals. Self-discipline is like a magic spell that can help you deal with the challenges in your life.

For example, Julia has a big math exam coming up, and she really doesn't feel like studying, especially since she doesn't really enjoy math. She's tempted to binge-watch her favorite TV series in the time she's supposed to be studying. However, she realized if she studied now, she would get better grades, which would mean more free time later. So, she resisted the urge to watch TV and she poured her energy into studying.

Don't think that being self-disciplined means you can never have fun. You simply need to find the right balance.

For example, your friends invited you to a lazy day at the beach or a barbecue at one of their houses, but you've promised yourself to exercise regularly and lead a healthy lifestyle. With self-discipline, you'll get up a little bit earlier and make sure you get some time in for exercise before you join your friends. You could even tell your friends that you should make your day at the beach not so lazy, and do some fun sport like volleyball.

Think of self-discipline as building your mental muscles. Just like your favorite athletes work hard to improve their skills, you can work on your self-discipline muscles. Let's say you want to learn a new language. It might feel challenging at first, and you'd rather switch back to your native tongue. But with self-discipline, you practice regularly, and soon enough, you're chatting like a pro with native speakers!

You're never too young to learn to lead a healthier lifestyle, and self-discipline can help you make healthier choices. Imagine your friends offer you sugary snacks, but you know it's better for your body to choose something nutritious. You use your self-discipline to choose a juicy apple instead of a sugar-packed treat.

So, how can you unlock the superpower of self-discipline? Well, it's all about practice and patience. Start small, set achievable goals, and celebrate your victories along the way. When you stumble, don't beat yourself up; just dust yourself off and keep going!

Journal Prompts

1. Think about a time when you struggled with self-discipline. Why did you struggle, and what can you do in the future to avoid these types of struggles?
2. What type of distractions interfere with your self-discipline? What can you do to deal with this?
3. Think about a time when you were successful at being self-disciplined. What were the positives, and how did it make you feel?
4. What habit would you like to learn or break to improve your self-discipline?
5. What skill or talent do you think you would like to improve? Can you put a routine in place to develop your skills?
6. Do you have any time-wasting activities or a tendency to procrastinate? Think about ways you can use your time more effectively.
7. Think about a time when you failed at something because of a lack of self-discipline.

What were the lessons you learned, and how did this improve your self-discipline?

8. What temptations do you face, and how can you deal with them, e.g., not buying junk food?

9. Have you managed to change some of your habits to more positive ones, e.g., instead of scrolling on your phone every night, you now read a book?

10. Do you face any barriers that make you want to give up when it comes to achieving your goals?

In the next chapter, we're going to have an autonomy lesson and discover some interesting things about the intricate relationship between your brain and body. I wish I had been taught some of these things when I was a teenager, as everything would have made so much more sense then.

We need these selfies to have a fulfilling life; however, just by knowing these definitions, we're not going to gain these qualities.

In the next few chapters, we are going to learn some techniques that will help us gain those qualities for an awesome life.

2

YOUR BRAIN AND BODY WORK FOR YOU!

W elcome to the roller-coaster ride of emotions and thoughts! We're going to take you on an exciting journey through the fascinating world of how your brain and body work together. Every emotion and thought you experience has an impact on your body and brain and shapes your entire life experience. So, strap yourself in, and let's get going.

In this chapter, we'll look at your body's super communication highway, mainly your nervous system. Think of it being almost like the Wi-Fi of your body. When you feel certain emotions, speedy messages will travel along this network and activate different parts of your body and brain.

Always remember that you're in the driver's seat when it comes to the wild ride of dealing with your thoughts and emotions and how they impact your body and brain. If you understand all the chaos involved, you can navigate all the ups and downs with a greater sense of control. Stay tuned for the exciting information that's about to be revealed.

WHAT'S GOING ON IN YOUR BRAIN?

So, let's start by taking a look at the fascinating world of your brain. We're going to look at the mystery behind your prefrontal cortex, that powerful part of your brain that helps you to be the smart and awesome person you are.

The prefrontal cortex helps you with all kinds of things, such as:

- It can help you make the smartest decisions, such as if you should save your money or splurge it on a new game.
- Your prefrontal cortex is there to help if you need to solve tricky math problems or if you're working on a project with many complicated angles, such as creating a presentation.

- Your prefrontal cortex is like your personal event planner; it can help you plan your day, week, and even your long-term goals.
- It also helps you concentrate when it comes to acing the test or learning a new skill. You will literally be laser-focused.
- We all get angry, upset, or anxious. Your prefrontal cortex will step in to help you keep your emotions balanced.

Something else that's very interesting to know about your prefrontal cortex is that it won't be fully developed until you're in your early to mid-20s. That's why you're sometimes impulsive and could end up making decisions you regret later. Don't worry too much about this. It's simply part of the learning process.

Next, let's take an interesting look at the world of the limbic system. This is where your emotions and memories take center stage. The limbic system is a powerhouse when it comes to your feelings and experiences. All the juicy stuff happens here!

LIMBIC SYSTEM

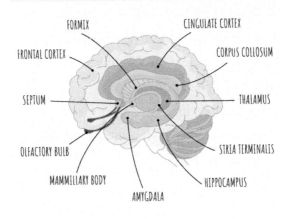

FORNIX
CINGULATE CORTEX
FRONTAL CORTEX
CORPUS COLLOSUM
SEPTUM
THALAMUS
OLFACTORY BULB
STRIA TERMINALIS
MAMMILLARY BODY
HIPPOCAMPUS
AMYGDALA

The hippocampus is your mental diary. Anything cool you learn, whether it's a new song or interesting school work, is stored here. It will help you remember anything from your friend's birthday to where you left your mobile phone.

The amygdala is like an alarm system that's always on high alert. It takes charge when you feel emotions like excitement, fear, or happiness and sends signals to your body that can do things like giving you sweaty palms or making your heart race with excitement.

It's important to remember that your amygdala doesn't always get things entirely right. It might send you an alarm for something that's not really dangerous, like meeting new people or when you have to speak up in class. It's not nice to get unnecessarily stressed, but it's important to remember that it can be a bit overprotective when it comes to keeping you safe.

Your hypothalamus is a master regulator that controls your bodily functions like thirst, hunger, and your body temperature. It's like an orchestra conductor that makes sure a bunch of instruments play harmoniously together.

The hypothalamus also communicates with your body through messengers called hormones. When you feel certain emotions, the hypothalamus will release hormones to make your face blush or your heart race.

You can think of the limbic system as a roller-coaster ride of feelings and memories. It can become overwhelming, but as you grow and learn, your brain will be better able to handle it. You should learn to ride your emotional waves with confidence, as your emotions are what makes you uniquely you.

Changes in the Teenaged Brain

When you're a teenager, there are a lot of changes happening in your brain. This can be confusing, and you could struggle to understand why you think and behave in certain ways. People may even get angry at your moody behavior.

Your brain is like a cool work in progress, going through massive changes as it sets the stage for the next phase of your development. Your hormones will play an important role during this intense time that can feel like a roller-coaster ride. The brain also changes during this time, as the connections between your brain's regions are reorganized and strengthened, which will change the way you think, feel, and interact with the world around you.

There is also a good reason you're influenced so much by your emotions rather than reason and logic. This is because your prefrontal cortex will develop after your limbic system. Your reward processing center is also more sensitive, and that's why you might want to get involved in dangerous behavior.

With time and experience, the prefrontal cortex gains more control over emotions, leading to more thoughtful and balanced responses. Think of your brain as a masterpiece in progress, then sit back and enjoy the journey of becoming the incredible person you're meant to be.

THOUGHTS AND EMOTIONS

We talk a lot about thoughts and emotions, but what are they, really?

Thoughts and emotions are a dynamic duo, and they're responsible for how you feel every day. Thought can be like little chatterboxes in your head that are always talking to you about certain things. These beliefs, ideas, and opinions can come to you when you're awake and also when you're dreaming.

When you're busy doing your schoolwork, thoughts are like your little personal mental assistants. They can help you figure out your math problems, formulate an answer to that essay question, or decide what to wear.

Emotions give your life color and flavor. They can indeed create a colorful painting on the canvas of your life by making you feel happiness, excitement, anger, or nervousness before the important events in your life. Pay attention to them, as they can give you an indication if you're on the right road in life.

Thoughts and emotions are kind of like friends who hang out together and influence each other in different ways. If you have positive thoughts, such as that you're capable of doing something, you'll feel happy and confident emotions. If you have negative thoughts and think you won't be able to do something, your emotions will be sad and frustrated.

It's important to realize you've got the power to manage your thoughts and emotions. You can choose which thoughts you want to listen to and which ones you want to ignore. If you can steer your thoughts in a positive direction, you can boost your emotions and really feel like a champion.

You can change your emotions in the following ways:

- Change the external situation that is making you angry, anxious, or whatever other unpleasant emotion you may be feeling. For example, you might be scared that you're going to fail an exam, but you can prevent this outcome by studying harder.
- You can shift your attention by choosing to focus on a more positive aspect of a situation. For example, it takes you a long time to get to school every day since you have to take the bus. You think it's a waste of time, as you could have spent a longer time sleeping. However, your friend suggests that you should use your time to study on the bus or catch up on your reading.
- Re-appraise a situation that's making you feel negative. For example, don't see an exam as measuring your worth as a person, but regard it as an opportunity to learn something. If you make mistakes, you'll know what you still have to learn and how you can do better the next time. We're all human and make mistakes as

long as we learn from them and improve from there.

- You can also use a technique such as mindfulness to keep you focused on the present and to make you feel calmer and more resilient.

Tom was becoming increasingly anxious as his exams approached. The fear of failure was casting a shadow over his days.

He shared his feelings with his girlfriend, who offered to share some tricks with him. She also told him he could get control of his emotions by taking action. If he studied harder, he would be able to regain control. She helped him shift focus. Tom used public transport and she told him that he should consider using the time he spent on the bus to study or read, as this would make him feel more productive.

She also said he should see exams as chances to learn and not as tests of his worth. Mistakes could be his stepping stones.

She told him he should stay calm and breathe deeply. Tom followed his girlfriend's advice, and on exam day, he was still nervous, but he felt more in control.

When he received his results, he was overjoyed to find that he'd passed everything and had even improved in a tough subject.

As he celebrated with his girlfriend, Tom realized that with the right tools, he could steer his emotions away from negativity. He could change his perspective, even in the face of adversity.

What's Getting on Your Nerves?

Your brain is wired with something called a "negativity bias," which means you'll focus more on negative experiences than positive ones. Your brain automatically gives attention to something that feels like a threat or a problem.

For example, you could get 18 answers correct in a math test of 20 questions. This is an excellent result, but your brain brushes off the right answers, and you find that you keep thinking about your wrong answers and do not understand how you made these mistakes. In the end, you think that you're not as smart as you really are, and your self-confidence takes a knock. This could also happen in social situations, e.g., a fun party where you meet some fantastic new people, but you keep focusing on the one negative comment about your clothes that you received from someone who has never liked you that much. In the end, your evening ends up being ruined because you can't stop thinking about this.

There's actually a good reason for this type of bias. It's a survival mechanism that has kept our ancestors safe from danger; their brains learned to focus on threats to help them stay alert and avoid harm.

However, the negativity bias can cause problems for us in today's world. It might cause us to feel unnecessary stress and also criticize ourselves. For example, we could have the same reaction to a math exam that our ancestors had to a threat to their lives, so you can see how this is an overreaction. We can actually train our brains to deal with this by being aware of our thoughts and actions and practicing to think in more positive ways.

When you get stuck in a cycle of negative thinking, try not to think about it too much. Try to think about the things you did right and the positive experiences you've had.

You have the power to decide how to respond to your emotions and to keep a positive and balanced outlook.

Sympathetic and Parasympathetic Nervous Systems

Maybe you've heard about the sympathetic and parasympathetic nervous systems (SNS and PNS), and you're wondering how these work exactly. Well, you're about to learn more as we dive into the marvelous world of nervous systems.

These two are like best friends, and they work together to help you face whatever life should throw your way, even the unpleasant things.

When you have a big exam coming up, the SNS will pump you full of adrenaline and get you ready to jump into action. Your heart can start racing, you will breathe faster, and energy will surge through your body. It's almost like getting ready for an exciting adventure.

At the end of the exam, your PNS brain will kick into action. It helps us relax and become calmer. Your heart rate will slow down, your breathing will be steadier, and you can take a sigh of relief. This would be your reward after overcoming the mighty exam dragon.

These two systems usually work together in balance. When the SNS is operating, the PNS will be on break. You have to find harmony between them, almost like dancing to very fast music and swaying to slow ones.

Your SNS is a "fight or flight" system, which gets you ready to face challenges head-on. It's like a turbo boost that helps you face that math test or give a presentation. But when the pressure's off, the PNS steps in to give you that feeling of calmness and peace.

You can determine when the PNS takes over in your body. By practicing cool techniques like deep breathing, meditation, or even just taking a walk in nature, you can invite the PNS to take center stage when you're feeling nervous before an exam or in any other difficult situation.

HUMAN NERVOUS SYSTEM

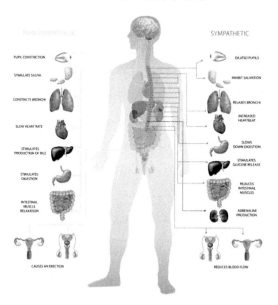

The Consequences of Stress When Your Fight or Flight Response Is in Overdrive

Stress can be like an overprotective bodyguard, which tries to keep you safe, but sometimes does its job a bit too well. When the "fight or flight" response goes into overdrive, it can mess with our bodies, which will have all kinds of consequences:

- Stress can make your brain feel like a scrambled Rubik's Cube—it can jumble your thoughts, and you may struggle to focus on anything at all. Say hello to brain fog.
- Stress can give you the "butterflies" or make your tummy go on a wild ride. It can even feel like there's a rollercoaster in your stomach during times of severe stress.
- Your heart could race like you're taking part in a marathon.
- Stress might play hide-and-seek with your sleep, making it hard to catch those Zs when you need them most. Stress can make sleep seem like a thing of the past.
- Stress can also give you acne breakout, not a give that you really want.
- Stress can also cause you bathroom drama. Your bladder might feel like tiny water balloons that are constantly about to burst.

- Stress can also be a massive pain in the head and surprise you with an unpleasant headache when you least expect it.
- It could also feel like your immune system is on vacation, as you can be more prone to sniffles.
- Stress could also cause issues with the reproductive system, unbalancing your hormones and causing your periods to go haywire.

In the next chapter, we're going to take a journey into self-discovery and building your self-esteem. It's just easier to manage your life if you've got a healthy dose of self-worth.

Your body and mind are a dynamic and interactive duo. If you believe in your self-worth, your brain will send positive signals to your body, which will respond by radiating positivity and confidence. If you doubt yourself, your feeling of worth will slip, and you may even experience an energy slump.

Remember that self-worth isn't about being perfect; it's just about being authentic and living a life that's true to your values and beliefs. You need to be able to accept yourself with all your quirks and uniqueness.

OWN IT: OWN YOUR WORTH

Well, let's take our first steps into something ultra important: recognizing how incredible and talented you are. This journey is going to be all about you because you deserve all the love and respect in the world, and you're the first person who has to give this to yourself. If you want others to accept and respect you, you need to own your worth. Walk with us as we unravel the secrets of self-esteem and self-acceptance.

You need to be your own biggest fan in life because you're the one who needs to motivate yourself to do things and get ahead in life. Cheer yourself on, and embrace all your talents. Do you love and respect yourself enough? Treat yourself with kindness, the same as you would your best friend.

Accept your imperfections, as they are what makes you so beautifully human. The secret to a meaningful and successful life is to keep going when things go wrong and forgive yourself for making mistakes, even potentially big ones. Self-esteem is truly like a superpower, and it's what helps you stand tall, deal with challenges, and grow in resilience.

Don't worry about fitting in; you were actually meant to stand out. Maybe you feel you're too weird, and that's why you don't have as many friends as you would like. However, this is actually the magic that sets you apart. So, embrace your confidence and let your uniqueness sore.

PROTECTING YOUR "SELF"

One of the most important ways to protect your "self" is to learn to stand strong against bullies.

So, what is the difference between a simple fight and bullying? A fight could simply be two people disagreeing on the playground, shouting at each other, and even pushing each other around. A bully uses their words and actions to do you real harm. Sometimes, they'll even target you for silly reasons, just because they've decided they don't like the way you look or how clever you are, or they simply don't like you for being you. You don't have to be their punching bag. You have the right to live your own fantastic story as a unique individual.

You get different types of bullying. You've probably encountered a few of them in your school and it's vital to know what they are so that you can handle any bullying.

Verbal bullying might not sound that serious, but it can sure hurt when someone yells at you or spreads mean stories or rumors about you. Words can hurt, but you have the power not to let them define you.

Physical bullying can have serious consequences, as the person getting bullied could be injured. This could include kicking, hitting, shoving, and even spitting on someone.

Giving someone the silent treatment is also a form of bullying. Maybe you've experienced someone trying to control you in that way before by ignoring you and trying to make you feel invisible.

Exclusion happens when someone leaves you out of a group intentionally. That's also bullying because you deserve to be included and valued.

Cyberbullying is a more recent development, but it's becoming increasingly common as the digital world becomes a real playground for bullies. As you probably know, cyberbullying happens online. It can involve nasty comments and embarrassing pictures of you shared without your consent, and you could receive hurtful messages. In this case, the "brave" villains are hiding behind their screens.

Handling Bullies

Unfortunately, bullying can affect you in all kinds of bad ways, and it's important to know the signs. You need to be able to handle your own emotions, as well as the bully.

Bullying can be like a rollercoaster ride. The one moment you're still feeling great, but then the bully turns up, and your mood plummets. It's tricky to be happy if you have to deal with ongoing negativity.

Bullies can have a negative effect on your attempts to build up social connections, as they often spread rumors and turn friends against each other. Even girls can be bullies, and they're especially good at sabotaging friendships by spreading false stories.

Bullying can also make it difficult to concentrate on your schoolwork, as constantly thinking about it will affect your concentration, and you could find yourself distracted in a very important exam.

Being bullied is also bad for your health and you can experience physical health symptoms such as headaches and stomachaches. Ongoing bullying can really drain your energy and vitality.

The bully's words can cause you to start doubting yourself and your self-confidence may take a knock. You're afraid of going to school or attending social events because it could feel as if the bully is hiding around every corner.

With the right strategies, you can overcome bullying. Your victory will make you stronger and more resilient and will help you deal with whatever comes your way.

It may not be easy to deal with bullies, but it can be done. After all, you don't want to spend some of the best years of your life living in fear of bullies.

So, how do you deal with these unpleasant individuals?

First of all, you need to hang on to your confidence because their main power comes from making you doubt yourself. So, keep on reminding yourself of how awesome you are, and don't let their mean words and actions penetrate your self-confidence. It's also important to remember that it's not your fault that you're being bullied.

When you're being bullied, it helps to have friends who have your back. Surround yourself with positive people who appreciate you for being you.

Play mind tricks with your bully to throw them off track. When they try to provoke you, treat them with kindness and rebuff their negativity with a witty comeback or simply a smile. Use your charm to deflect their attacks.

Try to stay as positive as possible and engage in self-care. Do the things you love doing, such as painting, reading, playing music, or even more crazy stuff like skateboarding.

Don't try to deal with bullying alone, especially not when it becomes physically threatening. Report the situation to adults you trust, like teachers, a school counselor, or even your parents.

Sometimes, it can work to ignore bullies. If a bully shouts insults at you, ignore them and walk away. This might make some of them mad, but others will leave you alone if they see you have the confidence not to respond to them. It's also a good idea to avoid places you know where the bully hangs out.

Am I the Bully?

Is it possible that you could be a bully without realizing it? This could be true if you're short-tempered, you get angry easily and disagree with people, and you tend to be manipulative.

Think about how you speak to other people. If your words cause a whirlwind of negativity and people get upset, it's probably time to rethink the way you speak to others. This is also the case if you feel powerful when you're making others feel small.

If you tend to exclude certain people from activities or groups because you don't like them, remember that you could be dooming them to loneliness. It's important to be friendly to everyone and make them feel included.

Teasing others can be fun, but if your jokes get too mean, it can hurt other people's feelings. Think before you say things to others, and make sure you're not being biased or prejudiced. You don't want to exclude others simply on the basis of their race, gender, or because of the way they look. People also don't always act or behave in the same ways, and it's important that we do our best to understand each other.

Maybe you're nice to others face-to-face, but your inner troll or bully comes out when you're in front of your computer. Perhaps you think you're protected when you spread negativity online, especially when you're using an anonymous account or one with a fake name. This is true to an extent, but you need to remember that you're insulting real people with real feelings.

Bullying can also happen almost unintentionally when you forget or struggle to put yourself in someone else's shoes to understand how they feel about something. Have you considered that not everyone will see things from your perspective? Before you say or do something to someone, think about how they might feel about it. How would you feel if someone did or said the same things to you? Don't treat someone else in a way you wouldn't want to be treated yourself.

Ultimately, it's up to you to choose what kind of person you want to be. It's so much more rewarding to change the lives of others for the better.

HOW TO SHOW YOURSELF LOVE AND RESPECT

You may think it sounds difficult, but you actually have the power within yourself to develop self-respect. It can be a bit of an adventurous journey, but it's better to start sooner rather than later.

You can travel on your self-respect journey in the following ways:

- Start by accepting yourself and creating your own character. Embrace your talents and uniqueness. Celebrate your uniqueness.
- Use positive thoughts as a type of armor to protect yourself against negativity. This armor will keep you strong when you have to deal with challenges at school or day-to-day setbacks.
- To keep motivated and moving forward in your school career and at home, you need to set goals that excite you. Learning new skills and doing the best you can in your exams can boost your confidence and self-respect.
- Build a strong support system of positive and kind friends who will lift you up.
- It's also important to keep your promises when you've made them to others and not waste people's time by making them expect things from you that you will never deliver.
- If you are grateful for the good things and people you have in your life, it will help you focus on the positive and give your self-respect a boost in the process.

- Practice bouncing back from disasters. Accept that you'll make lots of mistakes; it's all just part of how you'll learn and move up in life. It's human to make mistakes, and you should see them as growth opportunities.
- Use your voice, and speak up when you want to share ideas or speak out against something that you think is an injustice. Expressing yourself will not only empower others but also increase your self-respect.
- Be kind to others and spread positivity. This will not only help others but give you more self-respect in the process. Be polite to others. For example, let older people go first and help them by opening doors for them.
- Taking care of your personal image will also help you build self-respect. Be careful with how you dress, cover parts of your body that shouldn't be naked (don't be tempted to imitate certain celebrities who have body parts hanging out), and also respect the way others dress.
- Manage your emotions. You can show them, but always think before you speak and react.

Sally's Journey to Self-Respect

Sally, a high school student, wanted to stand out from the crowd and embrace her true self. She had a conversation with her friend Liam, who encouraged her to stand up for herself and accept her uniqueness. This became the catalyst for her journey to self-respect.

Sally acknowledged her own strengths and used her positive thoughts as armor against her negativity. She became more confident as she confronted her challenges with resilience. She also set academic goals and she surrounded herself with positive friends.

She also came to understand that it was important to treat others with kindness and empathy. Listening to Liam's perspective helped her use her voice to express her beliefs and stand up for them.

Activity: What Does Self-Love Look Like?

Embracing imperfection is a crucial step on the path to self-love and growth.

Nobody's perfect, not even those movie stars and celebrities who are your heroes and may end up disappointing you. Trying to be perfect at everything will just slow down your progress in life and can actually make you feel like you're stuck.

Today, we're diving into an empowering activity that will help you master the art of self-forgiveness. This activity is your chance to build your self-love and embrace your humanity. So grab a pen and journal, and start making notes.

Follow these steps to self-love:

- Find a quiet place where you can think without being interrupted. This could be in your bedroom or even somewhere outside. Set the mood with some calming music.
- Think about something that happened in the past for which you had to forgive yourself. Write a short description of what happened and how it made you feel.
- Write a reminder in your journal that it's fine to be human and make mistakes, e.g., "I'm allowed to make mistakes and learn from them."
- Imagine yourself as a character in a game that's taking part in some great adventure. If you have a friend playing the game with you, and they made quite a serious mistake, what would you say to them? Write down a compassionate message that you would give your friend. When you've finished writing, Replace your friend's name with your own and read it to yourself.
- Write a forgiveness letter to yourself. Focus on the situation for which you're forgiving yourself. Write with kindness and empathy, as if you're writing to one of your friends. In the

letter, you should explain to yourself that you deserve forgiveness and that you're letting go of resentment and guilt.

- After writing the forgiveness letter, take a deep breath and visualize releasing the negative emotions tied to the situation. Imagine them floating away, leaving you feeling lighter and freer.

- Reread your forgiveness letter when you feel you need a reminder to be compassionate to yourself. Think of it as a pep-talk that you can look at when you feel down.

How to Accept Compliments

Do you find it difficult to accept compliments, and you often brush them aside? It could mean that you're feeling insecure and you're afraid that you'll come across as being arrogant.

Even if you don't see yourself as positively as others, you can train yourself to accept compliments.

When someone gives you a compliment, thank them and accept it with a smile. It's not necessary to dodge or deflect compliments. Believe in your own awesomeness and don't try to brush off other people's positive opinions of you.

Try to think of compliments as magic potions that can boost your mood and self-esteem. Let the positive words of a compliment really sink in, and feel how the confidence surges through you.

When you receive a compliment, share your gratitude enthusiastically with your complimenter, as this will also make them feel good about themselves when you share your positive energy with them.

After you've accepted a compliment, be careful not to fall into the trap of self-doubt. Instead, focus on positive self-talk. You need to tell yourself that you deserve the compliment and that you're doing your best to boost your confidence.

Compliments can also be compared to treasure chests of positivity. The more compliments you give, the more you'll receive. Share compliments by being kind to others. You're sharing positivity if you compliment others.

Building Up Self-Confidence and Self-Esteem

Do you want to boost your self-confidence and feel like you're on top of the world? We're diving into some seriously cool activities that will give your self-esteem a boost. Get ready to unlock your inner superhero and rock your uniqueness like never before!

A Fantastic Visualization Activity

Make sure that you are in a quiet environment and that you have plenty of supplies for this creative activity.

Close your eyes, and make sure that you're completely relaxed. Imagine a portal from another world opening in front of you. Step through the portal into the place where you will find your best possible self.

Picture yourself as the best possible version of yourself. You're confident and positive as you stand tall in this vibrant landscape. What expression do you have on yourself? How do you carry yourself?

Imagine yourself thriving in different areas of your life. You manage the challenges in your life, accomplish your goals, and deal with your obstacles with determination.

Why Hire Me

This activity has two aspects:

- Write a confident cover letter to a potential employer. Be proud of yourself, and introduce your best possible self by focusing on your best qualities, accomplishments, and skills.
- Design a poster that shows your potential and your best attributes. Let your creativity loose

and use colors, images, and words that present the best version of you.

The Motivational Jar

This self-esteem-building activity is quite fun as well. It basically involves finding a jar or envelope or anything into which you can put pieces of paper. You could make it even more fun and creative by decorating the outside of the container with symbols, pictures, words, and whatever else you like.

Find motivational quotes and whatever else inspires you. It could be from movies, books, songs, or you could find them on Google. Write them down on pieces of paper, cut them out, fold them over, and put them into your motivational jar.

You should take a quote out of your jar at the beginning of each day. This will encourage you to think positive thoughts, and it will influence your optimism.

The Superhero Pose

We've all developed an interest in superheroes during childhood, but do you know the superhero pose?

The superhero pose can give you confidence and help you be more confident in life.

The superhero pose can be an instant confidence booster, and it's not difficult to achieve. It will help you feel more ready to take on the world, for example, if you have to do a nerve-wracking presentation in front of your class and you're scared people might laugh at you.

You can start by standing tall with your feet hip-width apart, your shoulders pushed back, and your chest out like you're just about ready to take on the world. Put your hand on your hips, or raise them in the air like you've just saved the day. Own your space, look and feel strong, and be ready to conquer what comes your way.

The superhero pose will trick your mind into thinking you are the one and that you've got what it takes to be a success. You'll feel awesome from the inside out.

Imagine you're about to give a presentation in class, meet new people, or face a challenge. Instead of slouching or hiding, stand tall like your favorite super-hero. You'll feel a surge of confidence flowing through you. And guess what? People around you will notice your confidence—it's like your body is sending out superhero vibes!

So, the next time you're feeling a bit nervous or unsure, channel your inner superhero. Strike that pose, show the world your confidence, and get ready to take on whatever life throws your way. Remember, you've got the power within you to be your own superhero!

Sentence Completion Activities

This sentence completion worksheet is a fun way to explore your inner world and to get to know more about your own emotions.

So, how does the sentence completion worksheet work? The idea is that you should come up with your own open-ended sentences, like "I want to achieve_____in my future."

Give it a go, and try coming up with your own sentences. Once you have a set of questions, take the time to do a daily check-in and answer one of your questions. You can write it down, type it out, or answer it in whatever way you choose.

Once you've been doing this for a while, say for two weeks, it's time to look back at your answers. Consider if you can detect any patterns or changes.

This exercise can help you in the following ways:

- The worksheet gives you a chance to express your thoughts and set them free.

- It can help you with navigating your emotions. You can use it like having a flashlight to guide you through the twists of your mind.
- The activity can help you understand yourself better and discover your own inner awesomeness.

Talking is one thing, but truly getting your thoughts across? That's a whole different ball game. Have your emotions ever felt so out of order that your thoughts were struggling to keep up?

Trust me, we've all been there. But a top-notch communicator can understand and manage their emotions. So, get ready to dive in and become the boss of expressing yourself when we look at emotional intelligence and empathy in the next chapter and how this affects our communication with each other.

4

OWN IT: W—WORK ON COMMUNICATION

Have you ever felt like your words are playing a game of hide and seek while you're struggling to control your emotions? Well, we're going on a journey that's going to level up your communication skills like never before. Yep, it's all about emotional intelligence, empathy, and finding your assertive voice. So, get ready to master these communication superpowers!

Working on your emotional intelligence can help you get a grip on your rollercoaster of emotions. If you understand what exactly is going on in your head, you can become a laid-back master of your emotions. In this chapter, we'll do a deep dive into emotional intelligence, which will help you understand why you feel the way you do and exactly what to do about it.

BUSTING THE MYTHS ON EMOTIONS

Once we've exposed all the myths that have been floating around about emotions, you'll see them in a whole new light.

Myth 1: Showing emotions is a sign of weakness.

Time to set the record straight: Showing emotions doesn't make you weak—it makes you human! Imagine how boring a superhero movie would be if the hero never showed any emotions. Emotions can help you understand yourself and connect with others. Crying, laughing, getting excited—they're all part of the awesome rollercoaster of life. So, next time someone tells you that showing emotions is weak, just remember that it takes strength to be real.

Myth 2: Emotions are useless.

Emotions might seem like random background noise, but they're actually the main characters in the story of your life. Emotions are like the compass that guides you through situations. Are you feeling nervous before a big test? That's your brain's way of telling you something is important. Your emotions are like signals that help you understand what's going on and how you can respond.

Myth 3: A feeling must make something true.

Have you ever had a gut feeling that turned out to be way off base? Here's the deal: just because you feel something doesn't mean it's always true. Emotions can be like those optical illusions—they make you see things differently, but it's not always reality. Trust your emotions, but also think things through. Be wary of your emotions, as they may throw you a plot twist from time to time.

Myth 4: A feeling about something must make the right decision.

Just because you feel strongly about something doesn't mean it's the right path to take. Emotions can be loud, but they're not always the best navigators. Think about it: Sometimes you're super excited about a game, but it turns out to be a total flop. Emotions are like your hype squad, but you also have to weigh them against facts and logic.

Myth 5: We should all have the same emotions about situations.

Your emotions are as unique as your favorite playlist. It's totally okay to feel differently from your friends. Imagine if everyone felt the same way about everything —that'd be like living in a black-and-white world! Emotions add color and depth to life. Your friends might not share your enthusiasm about a new movie, and that's perfectly fine. Embrace your emotions, and leave others to deal with theirs.

Myth 6: Without extreme emotions, life would be boring.

While extreme emotions can be like fireworks, everyday emotions are like the cozy blankets that make life comfortable. Imagine feeling angry 24/7—that's not exactly pleasant or comfortable. Calm emotions can be just as useful as extreme emotions.

Myth 7: Acting on intense emotions impulsively gets more done.

While intense emotions might feel like rocket fuel, zooming into action without a plan will only cause you to crash. Think about it: Texting a fiery message when you're mad can only cause things to blow up and cause further negative emotions. Emotions can burn you if you're not careful. So, think before you do something impulsively.

The Purpose of the Eight Primary Emotions

We often believe there are good and bad emotions, and we're also taught this from a young age. However, this isn't true, as each emotion actually gives us a unique message.

1. **Happiness** is like a spotlight on the things that make your heart dance. Its purpose is to show you what's going right and to encourage you to keep doing more of it.
2. **Sadness** has an important purpose—it helps you process loss and change. It makes you realize that you can let go of things that might not be working for you anymore.
3. **Fear's** purpose is to keep you safe. It's like a built-in alarm system that alerts you to potential danger. Instead of running away from fear, listen to its message and deal with the situation. Fear is your survival buddy that will help you make smart choices.
4. **Anger's** purpose is to highlight situations that go against your values or boundaries. It tells you that something isn't right. Instead of exploding, channel your anger into making positive changes and setting boundaries.
5. The purpose of **disgust** is to keep you away from things that could harm you—whether it's something physical or even toxic relationships. It reminds you to stay true to what's good for you.
6. **Surprise** is like a reset button for your brain. Its purpose is to help you process unexpected events and gather information quickly.

7. **Contempt's** purpose is to protect your self-esteem and boundaries. When you feel contempt, it's your inner defender speaking up when you're disrespected or treated unfairly. Contempt protects you and reminds you of your worth.

8. The purpose of **enjoyment** is to encourage you to explore, engage, and experience life fully. It's like a nudge telling you to embrace new adventures and enjoy the good parts of life.

Remember that emotions aren't here to label you or make you feel guilty—their purpose is simply to act as your guides. Instead of stuffing them away or judging them, take a moment to listen to their messages. So, next time you feel an emotion, think about what it's trying to tell you. You can regard emotions as the map to understanding yourself and the world around you.

CONTROLLING YOUR EXPLODING EMOTIONS

Are you wondering how to handle your intense emotions and ride the emotional wave? It can be scary, but with the right skills, it's entirely doable. Adolescence can be a confusing time, and your life could feel like a roller coaster of emotions. Sometimes, you feel deliriously happy, and then all of a sudden, you're upset. It's okay to feel this way, but it can help you a great deal to know how to handle your emotions.

Think of these changing emotions as waves, and you need to know how to ride them. You can control your emotions in the following ways:

1. When a strong emotion hits you, take a moment to pause and take a few deep breaths. Deep breathing can help calm your mind and slow down intense feelings.
2. Sometimes, naming your emotions can help you understand them better. Figure out what you're feeling; are you angry, anxious, or sad?
3. Emotions are like rising and falling waves. You should give yourself time to feel them without reacting immediately. This will help you to avoid saying or doing things that you might regret later.
4. Find a healthy way to let out your emotions. You could talk to a friend, write in a journal, draw, or even go for a run. Expressing your feelings can help you feel better.
5. If there's something causing your intense emotions, think about how you can deal with the situation. Is there a way to solve the problem? Can you talk to someone about it? If you can find solutions to your problems, it can

give you a sense of control. It could help you to write down your thoughts and feelings.

Ben Rides the Waves of Emotions

Ben, a teenager known for his temper, discovered the power of emotional control with the help of his friend, Tina. When he told her about his emotional turmoil, she compared emotions to waves that rise and fall. She told him about certain techniques to manage his emotions, such as deep breathing and managing his feelings. Ben practiced these methods, and they taught him to pause and reflect before he reacted to something.

Ben followed Tina's advice after arguing with his brother. He allowed himself to feel emotions without letting them dictate his actions. Ben also felt that journaling helped him deal with his emotions. With time, he got better at dealing with his emotional waves and also getting more control over how he responded.

Your Emotional Triggers

So, you've probably all had those times when it felt as if your emotions went on a roller coaster ride. This could be a result of something called emotional triggers.

Imagine this: You're still playing your favorite game on your Xbox and you're feeling just awesome until someone makes a negative comment about your gaming skills. Your mood changes, and you're instantly annoyed and upset. That's your emotional trigger.

Triggers are your emotional triggers, and when they're pushed, they could make you react in a big way. While hearing your favorite song can make you happy immediately, certain situations or memories can set off a chain reaction of emotions, sometimes a lot more intense than you would expect.

There are ways you can understand and manage your triggers:

- You need to understand what sets you off. Is it certain topics or comments? You need to pay attention to what makes your emotions go from 0–100 real quick.
- A trigger that hits you can be like a spark. Take a deep breath and don't let it explode. Take the time before you react to something.
- Ask yourself why that trigger gets to you. Sometimes, it's not just about what's happening now but something from your past that's linked to it. Understanding this can help you handle it better. If you've experienced trauma in the past, this could often be a trigger for your future behavior. For example, if you had bullies in

your class who laughed at you when you did presentations, you may lack the confidence to do so in the future. If someone laughs when you're talking, you could lose track of what you're trying to say.

- Learn ways to calm down when you're triggered. It could be listening to music, drawing, going for a walk—whatever helps you cool down.
- If you're comfortable, talk to someone you trust about your triggers. Sharing what's on your mind could often make a huge difference.
- Mindfulness can help you be the boss of your thoughts. When you're triggered, try to focus on the present moment instead of getting swept up in the emotion.

Controlling Your Triggers: Maya's Story

A teenager called Maya was known for her quick temper and intense reactions. Small things caused her to throw tantrums and go into fits of anger. When she started losing friends, she realized she needed to do something about her behavior and that she had to get control of her emotions.

One sunny day, she found a self-help book about managing emotions at her local library. While reading the book, she read more about emotional triggers and how they worked. She realized she could behave better if she understood more about what triggered her.

She started writing in a journal, especially when she felt really emotional. She wrote down what happened, what she thought triggered her, and how it made her feel. Over time, she started to see patterns. She became aware that certain situations and words set her off more than others.

Now that she was more aware of her triggers, Maya was ready to put what she had learned into action.

When she felt triggered, she would take a deep breath and count to ten. This helped her to think before acting. She felt in control in a way she hadn't felt before. She also learned to look deeper into her triggers, and she realized that some of them were the result of early childhood experiences. She started talking to her family and her friends about these triggers, and she felt as if a weight lifted from her shoulders.

Maya also found activities that helped her deal with her triggers. She wrote in her journal, practiced yoga, and worked on painting. Finding an outlet helped her deal better with her emotions.

One day, Maya found herself in a situation that usually triggered her anger. But this time, she felt different. She remembered her breathing techniques, thought about the trigger's root cause, and decided to step away for a moment. She took a walk and listened to her favorite song. When she returned, she was surprised to find that she wasn't angry anymore.

Over time, people noticed that Maya had changed. She seemed happier and was more patient. Her emotions no longer controlled her. She inspired her friends and other people around her to gain control of their triggers and deal with their emotions in healthier ways.

Worksheet—Identify Your Triggers

Let's dive into understanding your emotional triggers. They're like hidden buttons that can make you feel all sorts of emotions. This worksheet will help you discover your triggers and learn how to handle them like a pro.

1. Trigger Tracker

Think about some recent times when you've felt really emotional—angry, sad, stressed, or any other strong feeling. Write down the situations, people, or things that you think might have triggered those emotions.

Situation/event:

_____

Trigger(s):

_____

Emotion(s) felt:

_____

2. Digging Deeper

Now, for each situation you listed, ask yourself why that particular thing triggered such a strong emotion. Are there any past experiences or memories connected to it?

Situation/event:

_____

Why did it trigger me?
(Example: Maybe it reminded me of a time when I felt left out at school.)

_____

3. Common Themes

Look at the triggers you've listed. Do you notice any common themes? It could be certain types of comments, specific places, or particular people. Write down any themes you spot.

_____

_____

4. Your Calm Zone

When a trigger sets off a wave of emotions, it can be like a strong storm in your mind. Write down a few things that help you relax and cool down when you experience a trigger.

Activity:

————————————————————————————————

Activity:

————————————————————————————————

Activity:

————————————————————————————————

5. Mindful Moments

Mindfulness is like a superhero power for handling triggers. When you're triggered, try doing the following:

- Focus on your breathing for 1 minute.
- Pay attention to the sensations around you— what you see, hear, and feel.

6. Talk It Out

Think about someone you trust—a friend, family member, or teacher. Imagine talking to them about your triggers. Can they help you deal with your triggers?

Activities For Emotional Expression

Sometimes, you just need to let your emotions out. There are various fun activities that can help you express what you're feeling. Who knows, your emotions could even help you create a masterpiece!

- Draw, paint, or create something that reflects your emotions. You might have a magnificent creative piece hiding somewhere inside you.
- Listen to music that matches your mood or put together a playlist that helps you process your feelings. You can also try writing your own songs or playing an instrument. You may even find that different types of music help you express yourself while you're painting, writing, drawing, or doing some kind of other creative activity.
- Physical activity can release built-up emotions. Go for a run, dance it out, or try yoga—it's good for your body and mind.
- Put on your favorite tunes and dance like no one's watching. If they are, act like you don't care. Let your body move freely, and feel your emotions in your body with each stop.

- Try deep breathing, meditation, or guided mindfulness exercises. These help you stay present and calm in the midst of strong emotions.

MAKING YOUR VOICE HEARD

Let's look at social communication in a way that's easy to understand.

You can think of social interaction as a dance between people. It's all about how we connect, talk, and hang out with others. When you're chatting with friends, playing a game, or just having a conversation, social interaction is happening. It's all the fun moments you share with others.

For example, imagine that you're at a party with your friends. You're laughing, telling stories, and listening to others. That's social interaction in action! It's all about how we connect with each other, have fun together, and build relationships.

Social cognition helps your brain understand what's going on in social situations. That's the ability you have to figure out if someone's happy, sad, or joking by their expressions and words. Your brain can help you understand feelings, intentions, and the vibe of the group you're with.

For example, imagine you're watching a movie, and you can tell if a character is happy, sad, or surprised just by looking at their face and body language. That's your social cognition helping you read emotions, understand intentions, and know how to react in different social settings.

Social cognition, pragmatics, and language processing are key to unlocking the mysteries of how we connect, understand, and communicate with each other. So, pay attention as we uncover more interesting information about these topics.

Social cognition is like having a special radar in your brain that helps you connect with others, know how they're feeling, and make sense of the world around you. It's a really cool skill that helps you navigate friendships, conversations, and all sorts of social interactions!

Pragmatics is like the rulebook for conversations. It's about using language in the right way, depending on who you're talking to and what you're talking about. Think of it as knowing when to be serious, when to joke, and when to take turns in a conversation. Pragmatics helps you talk smoothly, and it's also easier for others to understand you.

For example, imagine that you're at a party with your friends. The way you talk to your best friend will be different from how you talk to your teacher or someone you just met. That's where pragmatics comes in. It helps you know when to be serious, when to be funny, and when to take turns talking. It's like the secret code that helps you navigate social situations and have awesome conversations.

Language processing is how your brain takes in words, understands their meaning, and puts them together to make sense. It's like when you read a text message and instantly know what your friend is saying.

For example, when you're reading a book or listening to a song, your brain quickly turns those words into ideas and images in your mind. It's like magic—you see the story, understand the message, and feel the emotions all because of language processing.

Friends With an Unbreakable Bond

Maya, Leo, and Ava were all good friends who went to Sweet Valley High School.

The school was going to host their yearly carnival over the weekend, and an electric current of excitement was sweeping the students. Maya had always had keen social cognition, and she immediately picked up on the electric atmosphere. The contagious laughter and happy chatter made her feel connected to the crowd at the fairgrounds.

Leo walked around, enjoying the food stalls and the lively games. He decided to try a rather competitive game called Whack-a-Mole. As he joined the line, he observed the players and their body language. His sharp social cognition helped him identify the determined faces, the playful nudges, and the gleeful shouts of victory. With this insight and information his brain has gathered, he strategized his approach, taking his swings with calculated precision.

Their third friend, Ava, got excited when she found a storytelling booth and the storyteller was a character from her favorite book series. It was easy for her to understand the emotions woven into the storyteller's words.

Her language processing ability allowed her brain to turn the storyteller's words into ideas and images in her mind. It was almost like a magical ability—she could see the story, understand the message, and feel the emotions in the story.

When the friends got together for lunch after enjoying their separate activities, they all wanted to talk at the same time and be the first ones to tell their stories.

However, pragmatics allowed them to realize they should give each other turns to speak.

They continued sharing their experiences and taking the time to listen to each other. After finishing their lunch, they enjoyed the various activities of the carnival together.

COMMUNICATION STYLES

We all have different communication styles. Let's dive into four of them—passive, aggressive, passive-aggressive, and assertive communication—using examples that feel just like your everyday situations. We'll look at how each style works and help you understand how you can make your interactions go smoother and more respectful.

Passive Communication

You're a passive communicator if you tend to keep your feelings to yourself and not speak up even when you want to. You let others make all the decisions, and you don't express your thoughts or needs. It might lead to you feeling frustrated or unheard.

For example, imagine you really want to watch a certain movie with your friends, but you don't say anything and then end up watching a movie you didn't want to watch.

Aggressive Communication

Aggressive communication is when you express yourself in an angry or really intense way. You don't really consider others' feelings and you only focus on getting what you want, even if it upsets others.

For example, your friend accidentally spills some juice on your shirt. If you yell at them and say mean things, that's aggressive communication.

Passive-Aggressive Communication

This style is a mix of being passive and being aggressive. You don't tell people exactly what's bothering you, but you show your feelings in a sneaky or indirect way. This can be confusing for everyone involved. This could also involve gossiping and telling stories about people behind their backs.

For example, if your sibling borrows your stuff without asking, and you don't tell them you're upset, but you hide their things to get back at them. After they've borrowed your stuff several times and you didn't tell them that you don't like it, you suddenly yell at them.

Assertive Communication

Assertive communication is a balanced and confident way of expressing yourself. You're honest about your feelings and needs, but you also respect the feelings of others. You speak up for yourself, but at the same time, you're still considerate of the needs and feelings of others.

For example, you have a group project due, but your part isn't finished because others haven't done their share. Instead of getting angry, you calmly talk to your group, and you suggest solutions to them.

Communication Tips

You can improve your communication skills with the right habits:

- You need to know who you're talking to. If you're chatting with a friend, using chill language is cool, but when emailing your teacher, you shouldn't use casual language. Not everyone will understand your slang. So, you need to keep your audience in mind when it comes to getting your message across.
- Guess what? Your body speaks, too, and can tell others a lot about you and how approachable you are, for example, if your body language is

open. Keep your arms relaxed and make eye contact to show you're tuned in. Even in video chats, look at the camera, not the screen. It makes a big difference.

- Spelling and grammar checks aren't perfect. To boost your communication game, you need to proofread your electronic communication messages before sending them. Be brief yet clear. After writing, step away for a bit, then read it like you're the receiver. If it makes sense, hit send.

- Sometimes it's better to phone someone, especially if you have a lot to say to them. Emails and DMs are good, but sometimes, a call works better. A back-and-forth conversation sometimes just flows better.

- Think before you talk. Treat everyone with respect and think about what you're saying. Taking a moment to collect your thoughts shows maturity and consideration.

- Keep a positive attitude and smile! Whether you're face-to-face or on the phone, a smile and a positive attitude will affect how you talk.

The Benefits of Using "I" Statements and How to Use Them

Using "I" statements can make it easier to talk about your feelings. It's about expressing yourself without making it seem that you're pointing your finger at someone else.

They have the following benefits:

- "I" statements can help you avoid unnecessary drama. Instead of sounding like you're blaming someone, you're just sharing how you feel.
- When you use these statements, you show others that you care about their feelings as well.
- When you use "I" statements, you don't make others feel attacked.

How to Use "I" Statements:

- Begin your sentence with "I." Like "I feel" or "I think."
- Describe how you feel. It could be "happy," "frustrated," "confused," or anything!
- Manage the situation that is bothering you and tell them how it affects you. For instance, "I feel stressed when we're late" or "I get overwhelmed during group projects."

So, instead of saying, "You're always late and it's annoying," try, "I feel stressed when we meet late because we might miss the movie."

FINDING YOUR VOICE WITH THE OPPOSITE SEX

Maybe you're wondering why it's important to have friendships with people from the opposite sex. It's important to be able to connect with the opposite sex and move beyond the stereotypes. It used to be thought boys and girls couldn't be friends, but we're all just human with our unique personalities. In fact, hanging out with the opposite sex will help break down gender myths. So, let's look at mixed-gender friendships.

Each gender has its strengths; girls might be great listeners and guys might have awesome problem-solving skills. Instead of competing, you should be building each other up and working together to make the most of your skills.

For example, you could be working together on a school project. The girls could get the brainstorming started and help people to get their ideas out there. To make the most of the project, it's vital that everyone's ideas get heard. When things get tricky, boys can use their problem-solving skills to save the day.

Instead of competing, you should be working together and collaborating. Compliment people when you see they're making the most of their strengths. Together, boys and girls can be ready to take on anything.

Another important aspect of getting along is to find things that you both enjoy doing. Boys and girls can do the same things, whether it's sports, hobbies, or movies.

Choose your friends well, and choose those who respect you and treat you well, regardless of their gender. You should worry more about the quality of your friends, rather than how many you have.

Stand up against peer pressure. Some of your friends may want you to hang out only with certain genders, but true friends will accept you for who you are and support your choices. You have the power to stand up for yourself and hang out with whom you want to hang out.

Remember to be authentic and sincere when you're around your friends of the opposite sex. True friends are comfortable with each other and sincere.

You should be able to confide in your friends, regardless of their gender. Good friends will listen to you and give advice, no matter what.

These days, we love to communicate electronically, but there's still magic in face-to-face communication.

Emojis on your cell phone or tablet can't always stand in for real emotion.

Just imagine your best friend's laugh or the way they raise an eyebrow when they're teasing you. You can't feel those things through a text or a snap. Face-to-face is for sharing expressions, vibes, and even those hilarious inside jokes that make you crack up.

Texting may be quicker, but nothing beats the energy of being in the same room. It's also a chance to practice all those awesome communication skills you've been building. You're nailing eye contact, active listening, and those subtle gestures that show you're totally tuned in.

So, while tech is cool, don't forget the real-life hangouts. Go to the park or just chill at home—face-to-face time is where the real magic happens. You'll be creating memories that emojis can't even come close to.

Step-By-Step Guide for Starting Conversations

Step 1: Be yourself.

It's essential to be your authentic self. Don't pretend to be someone you aren't and be confident in yourself.

You just need to be the awesome person that your friends believe you are.

For example, imagine you love books, but when you're talking to someone of the opposite sex, you feel you must impress them by pretending to be a movie buff. However, you've heard they like reading as well, so you decide to take a chance and stay true to yourself. You tell them you ran out to get the latest book of whatever writer you enjoy reading, and you spent the entire weekend reading. To your surprise, they share your passion, and you're able to have an authentic discussion about something you really enjoy.

Step 2: Choose the right time.

Timing is everything. Opt for moments when you both are relaxed and not too busy. Breaks, lunchtime, or casual hangouts can be perfect.

For example, you want to ask a girl out, but you need to find the right time to do it. You're busy with tests all day at school and you don't get the time to talk to her. During the lunch break, you notice she's sitting with her friends and having a good time. You decide not to interrupt their conversation but to wait for a better time.

If you choose the right time, she'll be more relaxed and more likely to agree to go out with you. You will feel more comfortable talking to each other.

Step 3: Make eye contact and smile.

If you give someone a genuine smile, it will tell them that you're friendly and approachable.

For example, you're at a school music event where a live band is playing. The music is loud, and you see someone you want to speak to, so you decide to make eye contact and give them a quick smile. The person returns your smile and you know this is code for asking you to start a conversation with them, even if it isn't immediately. It's a way of letting someone know you're ready to share good vibes with them.

Step 4: Begin with a friendly greeting.

Use a simple "Hi!" or "Hey there!" as a casual greeting.

It's often best not to overthink things and just start with a friendly greeting. Giving a casual wave and a smile can take the pressure off starting a conversation, and it can become easier just to start a chat. Don't worry about coming up with the perfect line; just be your awesome self and make the connection. You should keep things relaxed and real.

Step 5: Find a common interest.

Start with something you both might be into—a class, a TV show, or even a hobby. Shared interests give you the perfect excuse to start a conversation.

You're at a local community event, and you spot someone who seems pretty cool. You're thinking of striking up a conversation, and finding a shared interest gives you the edge.

You walk over and say, "Hey, I noticed you're checking out the art booth. Are you into painting, too?" You've tapped into a common interest—art—and you're interested to know if they share this interest. If they don't, you can always shift gear to something else. Finding common ground just makes it so much easier to start a conversation.

Step 6: Use open-ended questions.

Ask questions where people will need to give you longer answers and not just yes/no responses. For instance, "What do you think about this movie?" This keeps the conversation going.

Imagine you're at a friend's party, and you want to start a conversation with someone from the opposite sex. It's time to bring out those open-ended questions. Ask them if they've binge-watched any TV shows, and go from there. Open-ended questions are like doors to great conversations. You're inviting people to share more, and suddenly, you're talking about all kinds of exciting things, such as aliens.

Step 7: Listen actively.

Give them your full attention. Nod, show you're listening, and respond to what they say. It's all about having that genuine connection with someone.

You're at a local music festival, and you're chatting with someone who's interested in the same bands as you. It's time to practice your active listening skills. Show them that you're interested in what they have to say by nodding and smiling when they're talking about something interesting. Also, respond when they talk.

If you listen actively to someone, you're turning to their passions and interests. You're building a bridge of understanding with someone else.

Step 8: Share your thoughts.

Once someone answers your questions, share your own thoughts with them as well.

You're at a school event and you're talking with someone from the opposite sex who's really into basketball. You asked them about their favorite team, and now it's your turn to give your opinion. You find out that you support the same team and players.

When you share your thoughts, you're not just a great listener; you're also an active participant in the conversation.

The friendly back-and-forth will keep your chat balanced and interesting. You can turn a simple exchange into a full-on connection.

Step 9: Laugh at jokes and share laughs.

Humor is a great way of building bonds. If they crack a joke, laugh if it's funny. You can also make jokes or light-hearted comments.

You're hanging out at a friend's game night and you're striking up a conversation with someone who loves gaming, too. You end up making jokes about how you're always getting killed during various games like Fortnite.

By laughing at their joke and adding your own light-hearted comment, you're creating a fun, friendly atmosphere. Humor can make ordinary chats memorable. Plus, sharing laughs builds bonds and makes conversations feel more awesome.

Step 10: Respect personal boundaries.

Keep your conversations friendly and respectful. If the other person seems uncomfortable or isn't responding much, respect their space.

You're at a party and you start a conversation with someone from the opposite sex. You're talking about movies and music, and everything's going smoothly. But suddenly, you notice their body language changes— they're crossing their arms and looking around nervously.

You can show respect for their feelings by telling them that you can change topics if the discussion is making them uncomfortable. If you respect personal boundaries, you're aware of how the other person is reacting, and you can adjust a conversation if it takes an awkward turn. It's all about making sure both of you feel comfortable and at ease during a conversation.

Step 11: Keep it natural.

Conversations should feel like a comfy chat with a natural flow and not a rehearsed script.

You're at a neighborhood barbecue, and you're talking with someone from the opposite sex. Your conversation is going great, and you should let your natural flow take over now.

You laugh and share stories about a topic that's interesting to both of you. Instead of worrying about the next "perfect" question, you should let the conversation twist and turn naturally, almost like a river.

Step 12: Be mindful of body language.

Pay attention to your partner's body language during the conversation—if they seem engaged and interested, excellent! If not, it might be time to wrap it up.

When you're talking to someone of the opposite sex, and you notice they're leaning in, nodding, and their eyes are lighting up, it's a sign that they're engaged by what they're saying and they're interested in you. If they're fidgeting and looking around, they're losing interest.

If you are mindful of body language, you can ensure that both of you are enjoying the conversation.

Step 13: End positively.

When you're wrapping up, say something like, "It was great talking to you!" It ends with a friendly tone and opens the door for future conversations. Make sure that they know you enjoyed their company and that you're looking forward to more interesting conversations down the road.

Confess—Were You Really Listening?

When having a conversation with someone, we all have those moments when we lose track of what they're saying or we miss what they've said because we just want to jump in with our own thoughts to tell them what we think of it all. However, active listening can help you fully appreciate what someone is trying to share with you.

You can do the following to level up your listening game:

- Start by putting all distractions away. Close TikTok, get out of Facebook, and put your phone away. This will help you focus fully on what the other person is saying.
- You don't have to take part in a staring contest, but you need to make eye contact to show you're part of the conversation.
- Give the speaker regular nods to show them you're listening and keeping up with what they're saying.
- Don't rehearse your response when someone else is speaking; otherwise, you're going to miss half of what they're saying. You're not a superhero who can predict what someone is going to say next.

- Let someone finish talking before you start with what you want to say. Don't interrupt someone while they're still mid-sentence. Let them finish their thoughts.
- Tune into the tone and emotions of the person who is speaking. Sometimes, you'll have to read between the lines to find the truth of what they're really saying.
- Share their excitement and ask them to tell you more about a specific topic.
- Use "I statements" to show them you're sharing their experience.
- Don't rush in to fill someone else's silence. People sometimes need to gather their thoughts. It's like waiting your turn in a game.
- Show support once you're aware that someone has stopped speaking by using comments such as "That sounds like a lot to handle."

Talking About the Hard Stuff

Boundaries are about protecting yourself, your feelings, and your well-being. They can be a game changer for the following reasons.

Think of your emotions as your safe family home. Boundaries are like the walls of your house—they keep out anything that doesn't belong there. Setting boundaries helps you protect your feelings from getting hurt by people who might not understand or respect them.

Boundaries can also keep you safe from situations where you could be harmed emotionally, physically, or mentally. For example, as you wouldn't jump off a cliff without a parachute, you shouldn't let someone cross your boundaries and make you uncomfortable.

Boundaries are like your personal rulebook. They tell others how you want to be treated, and they set the tone for healthy relationships, and you indicate to others that you won't settle for less.

Setting boundaries is important for a healthy mind. It's almost the same as eating healthy and exercising to keep your body healthy. It prevents you from getting overwhelmed, stressed, or anxious by giving you the space you need to breathe and relax.

It's almost like when you learned to ride a bike. Setting boundaries is a skill you're going to use forever. It could be with your friends and family or for a job you'll have in future, but knowing how to set boundaries will help you to be successful in life.

So, how do you go about setting your boundaries? Well, you can start by recognizing your feelings and listening to them. If something doesn't feel right to you, it's a sign that you need to set boundaries.

Consider things that are unacceptable to you and that make you upset. These are the areas where you need to set boundaries.

You also need to set boundaries in the online space. Don't share your personal information, and be sure to block whoever makes you feel uncomfortable.

Use key phrases to communicate your boundaries. If you don't like the way you're being treated, tell people this. Give them the rulebook of how you want to be treated.

Healthy and Unhealthy Boundaries

Boundaries can be healthy or unhealthy. Let's look at a few examples.

Healthy Boundaries

Healthy boundaries can be regarded as the following:

- You tell your friends you need time to recharge, and they respect your feelings.
- You share your thoughts and feelings with a friend, and they listen without judging you.
- You communicate your boundaries in a romantic relationship and your partner respects your limits.

- You protect your personal information online and you make sure your social media accounts stay private.
- When someone asks you to do something you're not comfortable with, you politely decline without feeling guilty.

Unhealthy Boundaries

Unhealthy boundaries can include:

- Someone is constantly invading your personal space, and it's making you feel comfortable.
- You're trying to talk to a friend or family member about something that's bothering you, but they dismiss your feelings and then change the topic.
- You could be pressured into doing something you're not comfortable with, which totally ignores your boundaries.
- You share too much personal information online without considering the risks to your privacy.
- You could be saying "yes" to things you don't really want to do, as you believe you should always be pleasing others.

Journal Activity—Setting Healthy Boundaries

In this journal activity, you'll take a look at different areas of your life where it's crucial to set boundaries and to create a roadmap to creating healthier relationships not only with others but also with yourself.

Instructions

- Start this activity by reflecting on your feelings. Think about moments when you felt uncomfortable, stressed, or upset. Reflect on what triggered these emotions and write a few notes about each situation. For example, maybe you don't like it when your friends borrow your stuff without asking.
- Think about the different areas of your life, such as relationships and digital interactions. Do you need to set boundaries in any of these to protect your personal well-being?
- Practice communicating your boundaries assertively and respectfully. Write down phrases you could use in various situations.
- Make a list of signs that someone is crossing your boundaries. Take note of your emotions, feelings, and behavior. For example, if you're starting to feel stressed, it might be a sign that someone is crossing your boundaries.

- One benefit of setting boundaries is that you're caring for yourself. Write down activities that help you recharge and take care of your emotional well-being. This could be anything from reading a book to going for a walk alone.
- Reread your journal entries regularly to check if they still reflect your feelings and needs. You should make adjustments where needed.

A SHORT GUIDE TO UNDERSTANDING BODY LANGUAGE

Body language is almost like a secret code that helps you understand what someone is really saying. You can decode their message, even when they're not using words.

Here's a guide to help you understand body language.

- Friendly eye contact shows you're interested and engaged. Your eyes could tell someone a lot about you without you actually saying anything to them. The trick is to give them a friendly look and not to try to stare them down.
- A smile can be interpreted as a universal sign of positivity. It's a way of letting people know you're friendly and approachable.

- An open posture, sitting or standing with your arms uncrossed and facing the person you're speaking to, shows you're open to the conversation.
- If you nod and lean in when someone's speaking, it shows you're genuinely interested in what they've got to say.
- If you mirror another person's body language, for example, crossing your legs when they do, it shows you're connected to them.
- If you're fidgeting or checking your phone when speaking to someone, it signals to them you're bored or uncomfortable. Focus and stay present to show you're engaged, that you like that person, and that you would like to hang out with them.

How to Say "No" Respectfully

We all need to say "no" at times, but this can be difficult to do, especially if we're scared of hurting someone's feelings.

You can say "no" respectfully in the following ways:

- Just be honest and direct. If someone invites you to an event that you don't want or can't attend, just tell whoever invited you that you can't attend this time.

- Provide reasons. For example, tell them if you already have a lot of other commitments on your plate.
- Suggest alternatives. If you can't attend a social event, suggest other times that you can get together.
- You could also turn down an invitation without directly saying "no." Just inform someone that you already have other plans or commitments or that you're focusing on something different at the moment.

Saying "no" is about taking care of yourself. You should never feel guilty for prioritizing your own well-being.

In the next chapter, we're going to take a more in-depth look at fear and anxiety. You've probably had fear and anxiety show up like unwanted guests in your mind. Fear can interrupt your plans to chase your dreams, and when it brings anxiety along for the ride, things just become so much more stressful. And we don't need that, as we already deal with enough stress from the world around us. You can use the next chapter as your secret weapon against fear and anxiety.

Let Others Know the Skills They Need to Connect With Others, Communicate their Needs Confidently, and Be the Masters of Their Emotions

"What we can or cannot do, what we consider possible or impossible, is rarely a function of our true capability. It is more likely a function of our beliefs about who we are."

— ANTHONY ROBBINS

Ever feel like life is a lot harder these days than it used to be? Do you wish it was as easy to make friends, do well at school, and express what you want and need? All the clarity and simplicity of childhood seem like worlds away, and it happens almost as quickly as you enter your teen years.

On the one hand, you know that you have what it takes to survive if push comes to shove. On the other hand, everyday challenges—such as starting a conversation with someone you don't know well, knowing how to keep your emotions in check when things get tense, and stopping bullies from getting the upper hand—can be daunting.

My hope is that by this stage in your reading, you are discovering that navigating the teen years successfully depends, above all, on one thing: the extent to which you hone the specific skills you need to thrive—skills like communication, conflict resolution, and expressing yourself assertively.

Another pretty bizarre thing about being a teen is that sometimes, all you want to do is sit in your room, listen to music, and daydream. It can be so much harder to let your parents and siblings know how you feel, and sometimes, even though you know you are loved, it can feel like nobody really understands what you are going through.

Know that you are not alone. The teen years are well-known for being a time of immense change, hormonal surges, and major brain development. And sometimes, you need a little "me time" to sort it all out and feel like you're on top of things.

If you find this book is already opening your mind to essential life skills you need to make the most of your teen years, I hope I can ask you to leave a short review on Amazon.

Share a bit about your own story, the skills you may be struggling with, and the techniques you have found to be most helpful.

As unbelievable as it may seem, even the most self-assured teens struggle with their thoughts and emotions.

Nobody is born with the full set of skills they need to shine socially and academically.

Becoming more confident, assertive, and resilient is part of an exciting journey that promises infinite rewards.

Please do your share to make it a little easier for other teens who need a little guidance so they can make the most of this unique time in their lives.

Scan the QR code below

5

OWN IT: N—NAVIGATE FEAR AND ANXIETY

L ife's like a playlist with awesome beats and maybe a few unexpected skips. But sometimes those moments can get too intense and anxiety and stress could crash your party. We'll show you the secret mix that will help you deal with your fears, conquer your anxiety, and dance your way through life.

THE OLD TECHNIQUES THAT REALLY CALM YOU DOWN

Imagine your body is like a high-tech control center with lots of wires and connections. One of the most important wires in this system is called the "vagus nerve." It's like a superhighway that starts from your brain, goes through your heart and lungs, and ends up in your stomach and other important organs.

The vagus nerve helps you manage how calm or excited you feel. It helps your body go from "chill mode" to "active mode" and back again. Your vagus nerve will help you feel better when you're anxious or stressed out.

To explain in simple terms, it works like this:

- The vagus nerve connects your brain to your feelings. When you're worried or scared, this nerve tells your brain to relax.
- When you're feeling nervous, the vagus nerve slows your heartbeat and helps you take deep breaths.
- Your vagus nerve is also involved in that "butterflies in your stomach" feeling. It helps your stomach and digestive system do their jobs properly. When you're stressed, it helps calm your tummy and makes sure everything keeps moving smoothly.

You can also try the following to give your vagus nerve a boost. Breathe slowly and take deep breaths in and out. This will help you relax.

If you splash your face with cold water, it can also give your vagus nerve a boost to help you relax. Gargling water and singing loudly can also give your vagus nerve a workout.

Laughter is great when it comes to activating your vagus nerve. So watch a funny movie, or spend some time with friends who make you laugh.

Leading a Less Stressful Life

Life can sometimes feel like a roller coaster ride with lots of twists and turns. But always remember, you've got the power to make life easier for yourself.

The first thing you would need to do is to identify your problem and tackle it. Think of your stress as a puzzle. You will have to figure out all the pieces of this puzzle. Are there pieces for school stuff or drama with your friends? When you know what is bothering you, you can work on finding solutions. Talk with a friend, family member, or a counselor who can help you figure out the pieces of your puzzle.

Avoid stress—if you can do so. Think about it as being like the weather. You can't control the weather, but you can control how you react to it. For example, if it rains, you can wear a raincoat, or if it's very hot, you can wear shorts or a T-shirt. Always think if there's anything you can do to control the situation. If traffic makes you late for school, could you possibly take an earlier bus? You can't avoid stress, but you can take small steps to make your life go smoother.

Sometimes, we need to let things go to make it easier for us to deal with stress. You can picture your stress as your school backpack, and each worry you have is a rock inside it. The more rocks you have in your bag, the heavier your load. Now, take out the rocks that don't really matter. This would be the small things, such as not being able to find your favorite shirt. You should save your energy for more important things such as studying for your exams and spending time with your friends.

Relaxing doesn't mean you have to be a couch potato all day long, stuffing your face with chips while watching movies or sports. Of course, you could do that if you really wanted to, but you can also relax in an active way. It's all about doing fun things that make you happy and that you really enjoy doing. This could be active things like going for walks or the gym, running around with your dogs, or even doing some kind of craft. You need to give your brain a break so that you can tackle challenges with a refreshed mind.

Another excellent way to deal with your stress is to think of others. Contributing to the world and helping others can put a smile on your face. So, volunteer and spread the good vibes around. Even giving out compliments can give your happiness a boost. Knowing you're making a positive impact can also help you put your own problems in perspective.

Stress and Time Management

Managing your time can help you make sure you get your school work done on time and also that you turn up on time for that interesting movie you're going to see with your friends. Your friends might hold it against you if you're the one responsible for making them miss their favorite film.

The power of planning can give your time management a boost. You'll feel more in control and less overwhelmed when you plan stuff. Use a planner or an app to make notes of your school stuff and hangouts that you've got planned with your pals.

Having goals can also help you manage your time better. You've probably heard people talking about SMART goals. SMART stands for Specific, Measurable, Achievable, Relevant, and Time-Bound. (SMART Goals for Teens, 2022)

Instead of just saying, "I want to do better in school," try, "I want to improve my math grade by 10% in the next two months." These goals give you a specific target to work toward.

If you have a busy life, you've got to prioritize like a pro. Focus on the essentials first. There's no point in stressing about the big things last.

When it comes to big school projects, it could help you to break them down into smaller tasks. If you work on small pieces, it's easier to finish the entire project without becoming overwhelmed.

This is one of the difficult parts, but time management also involves saying "no." You simply don't have time to do everything or to please everyone. You have to protect your energy, so don't feel bad about saying "no" to things that make you feel stretched thin or don't align with your goals.

What Fears Are Playing On Your Mind?

We all have our fears, and sometimes they even develop into phobias. You've probably felt fear to the extent that your heart races and your palms get sweaty. Fear is a natural response to something that seems scary.

Fears are like warning nudges from our brains that doing something might not be the best idea. It's when you get that jittery feeling or butterflies in your stomach before you have to do a big presentation at school. Fears keep us on our toes and ready to tackle the challenges that come our way. Fears are common, and they can be healthy because they can help us do our best at school, for example, when we need to study for a difficult exam.

While a certain amount of fear is healthy, too much fear is unhealthy and can become phobias.

Phobias are a bit like fears in turbo mode. They're intense, irrational fears that go way beyond normal reactions. For example, being scared of spiders is a fear, but if you can't even look at a picture of a spider without feeling like you're going to faint, you're moving into phobic territory. Unfortunately, phobias can turn simple fears into absolute nightmares.

Fears and phobias can become a problem when they take over your life and stop you from doing things you need to do and which you used to enjoy doing. For example, if you have a social phobia, you could avoid going to parties with your friends or talking in class.

If you feel like fears or phobias have taken over your life, don't be scared to ask for help. A good therapist could help you deal with your fears. They can give you cool techniques to manage your fears, like gradual exposure therapy, where you face your fears bit by bit.

Breaking Past Your Fears

Life's an adventure and can be full of ups and downs, and often brings us face-to-face with our fears.

However, you can conquer your fears and be the hero of your own story. If you can face your fears, it brings you one step closer to the bold life you want to build for yourself.

Questions to Help You Become More Aware of Your Fears

The following questions can get you started on your journey to overcoming your fears. Answer them as comprehensively as possible in your writing journal. Take your time when you answer them, and be as honest as possible:

- What situations or scenarios make you feel uneasy or nervous?
- Are there any activities or places you avoid because of fear?
- Do you notice physical sensations such as a fast heartbeat when you're scared of something?
- Have you ever avoided doing something new because you were scared of failing?
- Do you overthink situations and imagine worst-case scenarios?
- Have you ever had a strong reaction to something that others seem to handle easily? What triggered your response?

- Are there any fears or worries that you've had for a long time? Have they changed over the years, or do they remain consistent?
- Do you notice any patterns in the types of fears you experience? For example, do they often revolve around social situations, specific animals, or specific activities?
- Have you ever confronted your fears, and how did you feel afterward?
- Will you seek support or guidance if your fears interfere with your daily life?

Climbing Toward Confidence With an Exposure Ladder

Each step you take on the exposure ladder is another step toward breaking free from your fears. This is the basis of an exposure ladder, a gradual approach to confronting your fears and anxieties. Just like a ladder can help you reach things that are out of reach to you, an exposure ladder can help you conquer things that are holding you back. Each step up this ladder will bring you closer to confidence and self-assurance. Whatever your fear, whether it is spiders or public speaking, the exposure ladder will help you challenge it in a safe and controlled way.

Activity

You can create your own exposure ladder to help you face your fears step by step.

You'll need paper, a pen or pencil, some sticky notes or index cards, and a supportive friend or family member if you need someone to take part.

The Rung of The Ladder

- Your first step should be to identify the fear you want to overcome at the top of your paper. This could be anything from public speaking to a fear of heights.
- Create a list of smaller steps that gradually expose you to your fear. These steps should start with something that is mildly uncomfortable and progress to more challenging tasks.

For example, if your fear is public speaking, your ladder might look like this:

Step 1: Speak in front of a mirror for 1 minute.

Step 2: Record yourself speaking and watch the recording.

Step 3: Practice speaking in front of a small group of friends or family.

Step 4: Speak in front of a larger group, like a class or club.

Step 5: Present a topic you're comfortable with to a larger audience.

You need to assign a level of discomfort to each step, from 1–10. The number "1" would represent mild discomfort, while "10" would be intense fear.

Okay, so you'll start the process like this. For now, you're standing at the bottom of the ladder, where your fears feel unmanageable to you. You start climbing, and with every rung you climb, you're stretching your comfort zone. The further you get up the ladder, the more you'll find what once was terrifying to you will become easier to do. When you reach the top, you'll have a newfound confidence to confront your fears.

So, practically, it will look like this:

- Write each step on a separate sticky note or index card. Arrange them from least to most challenging, creating your exposure ladder.
- Begin by facing the first step on your ladder. Spend time confronting your fear in a controlled environment. This could mean

practicing your fear or simply thinking about it in a safe space.

- You need to spend time with each step until you're able to decrease your discomfort level significantly. You could need to repeat a step several times before moving on. Don't worry if you feel you're progressing too slowly, as you need to progress gradually.
- Move on if you feel comfortable with your step. Expose yourself to more challenging scenarios as your confidence increases.
- If you find that you're struggling with some of the steps, get help from a friend or family member. They can encourage you and make the whole experience less scary.
- Reflect on your experience after each step. Write down your thoughts and feelings, and if a step is too overwhelming, you need to adjust it.

Life is about embracing the positive, overcoming the negative elements in your life, and becoming the amazing person you're meant to be. It's important to overcome challenges and find balance, but that's just the beginning of your journey. In the next chapter, we look at how you can turn your self-belief into positivity and achieve extraordinary success. Get ready to unleash your potential!

6

OWN IT: I—INTENTIONAL MINDSET SHIFTS

A t times, we all have a little negative voice in our heads that tells us we can't do something or that we won't be good enough at it. Well, we're now going to look at strategies that can help you build a mindset that is about growth, positivity, and lifelong learning. Flip your negative self-talk on its head, show gratitude, and learn to build resilience.

So, let's take the first steps to creating a fierce mindset.

WHAT DOES YOUR MINDSET SAY ABOUT YOU?

Let's take a stab at learning more about your mindset by doing this fun mindset quiz. The quiz is like a magic mirror that reflects how you see yourself and your abilities.

Instructions

For each question, circle the letter that best describes you. Once you're done, add up your scores to discover your mindset. Let's do this!

I'm born with my intelligence, and I can't really change it:

a) Totally agree 3

b) Agree 2

c) Disagree 1

d) Strongly disagree 0

I believe I can improve and learn more, even if I'm smart:

a) Strongly agree 3

b) Agree 2

c) Disagree 1

d) Strongly disagree 0

Being good at sports is mostly about natural talent, not effort:

a) Strongly agree 0

b) Agree 1

c) Disagree 2

d) Strongly disagree 3

I will get better at something if I put more effort into it:

a) Strongly agree 3

b) Agree 2

c) Disagree 1

d) Strongly disagree 0

I sometimes feel frustrated when I receive feedback on my performance:

a) Totally agree 0

b) Agree 1

c) Disagree 2

d) Strongly disagree 3

Feedback from people like parents, coaches, and teachers helps me improve:

a) Strongly agree 3

b) Agree 2

c) Disagree 1

d) Totally disagree 0

Smart people don't have to work hard; it comes naturally to them:

a) Totally agree 0

b) Agree 1

c) Disagree 2

d) Strongly disagree 3

I can improve my intelligence if I make an effort:

a) Strongly agree 3

b) Agree 2

c) Disagree 1

d) Totally disagree 0

My personality is fixed and not much can be done to change it:

a) Totally agree 0

b) Agree 1

c) Disagree 2

d) Strongly disagree 3

One reason I enjoy doing schoolwork is because I love learning new things:

a) Strongly agree 3

b) Agree 2

c) Disagree 1

d) Totally disagree 0

SCORE CHART

22–30: Strong growth mindset

17–21: Growth with some fixed ideas

11–16: Fixed with some growth ideas

0–10: Strong fixed mindset

MY SCORE: ____

MY MINDSET: ____

Remember, this quiz is a tool to help you understand your current mindset, and it's totally okay wherever you land. You can shape and evolve your mindset as you learn and grow.

Strategies to Develop a Growth Mindset

There are all kinds of strategies that can help you develop a growth mindset. Improving your decision-making and problem-solving skills is a particularly important one. The better you get at making smart decisions and solving tricky challenges, the easier your life will become.

A growth mindset is the key to unlocking your full potential. Imagine your mind as a garden that can flourish with the right nourishment. It's up to you to sprinkle the seeds of growth and make your own mind blossom.

Think of yourself as being a hero on an epic quest in your life. You have the power to shape your destiny, but you need to be able to make choices that align with your goals, values, and dreams. Your growth mindset will be the result of this process.

Lucy's Journey to a Growth Mindset

Lucy was a teenager with big dreams. She was cautious and tended to avoid risks. Lucy didn't enjoy taking part in challenges, and she liked being comfortable.

One day, Lucy's teacher announced that they were going to have a science fair at school, and she was very excited. However, she also felt doubt and fear, as she thought she wouldn't be good at it. They all received projects they had to do with the fair.

As weeks passed, Lucy found herself struggling with the project. She wanted to give up, but she carried on, as she thought she would be able to learn from it. Lucy asked her cousin Riley for help. She knew Riley had recently completed a series of difficult projects, and she was also a high achiever.

Riley told her that she saw challenges as an opportunity to learn. When she couldn't do something, she reminded herself that she would eventually be able to do it if she kept on working on achieving her goal.

Lucy began researching and experimenting and experienced some failures. She tried to embrace every failure as an opportunity for learning, even though she found it difficult, and she didn't deal well with criticism.

Her mindset changed with time. She came to see challenges as interesting puzzles, and her confidence increased with every success she experienced.

On the day of the science fair, Lucy was nervous about her project, but she was also proud of how far she had come and what she had achieved. People admired her work, and she also told them about her journey of gaining confidence and how she developed a growth mindset in the process.

Decision-Making and Problem-Solving

As part of our growth journey, we need to cultivate decision-making and problem-solving skills. Life is full of unexpected challenges that we need to conquer and we need to be able to seize opportunities. This is where decision-making and problem-solving skills come in. It's your catalyst for developing resilience and a growth mindset.

Try the following tips for solving problems and making decisions:

- Before you make a decision or try to solve a problem, you should try to gather as much information as possible. You can do your own research, but also ask your family, teachers, or even friends for advice. It often helps a great deal to speak to someone who has already been through what you're trying to figure out. For example, if you're interested in studying in a certain field after school, but you're not sure if it is the right one for you, try to speak to people who have already studied in this field.
- When you have to consider a few things, make a list of advantages and disadvantages. This can help you see the big picture of an issue and you'll be able to make a more informed choice.

For example, if you're struggling to decide whether you should go to a party with your friends or stay at home and work on an assignment, make a list of the advantages and disadvantages of doing both.

- Also, listen to your gut feelings when you're about to make a decision. While you shouldn't rely on your gut alone, your intuition could be a valuable guide, and you should listen to your instincts. For example, if you can't decide if you should go somewhere with someone alone, but you get a bad feeling about them, then listen to your gut instinct. It's always better to be safe than sorry.

- If you're faced with a seriously complex problem, don't panic, but break it down into smaller, more manageable parts. The problem as a whole will be less overwhelming if you address each part one at a time. For example, if you have to write a complex assignment, break it up into chapters or topics and face one at a time.

- When you're faced with a problem, it can often help to brainstorm different solutions. For example, if you want to study for a specific degree after you finish school that you can't afford, consider your different options. Can you take a loan, apply for scholarships, or work a part-time job to help you pay the fees?

- Think about the potential outcomes and consequences of your decisions. What are the negative and positive short-term and long-term consequences of your decisions? For example, if you don't study for your math test and go to a party, you'll fail your test, but you could have a good time with your friends at the party. In the long term, a failed test could drag down your grades for the entire year, although, on the social side, you might become more popular and be invited to more parties.

- You need to accept that making mistakes is a natural part of the process of learning and growing. If you made a decision that didn't turn out all that well, simply see it as an opportunity to learn and grow. For example, you didn't prepare properly for a presentation you had to give in class because you played an online game with your friend. As a result, you get a low grade and you're embarrassed. You deserve to feel a little bit bad about that, but hopefully, you've learned that you need to work harder in the future.

- A positive attitude can go a long way when it comes to dealing with challenges and coming up with creative solutions. For example, you're struggling to keep up with your studies, sports, and other extracurricular activities, but you come up with creative solutions where you can save time, such as doing extra work before school.

- After you've made a decision or solved a problem, you should always take the time afterward to think about what worked well or what you could have done better. For example, should you have spent more time working on the layout of your project? Maybe your information was excellent, but you lost grades because the layout wasn't neat and professional enough.

Maya's Growth Journey

Maya, an adventurous teenager, lived in a small town.

One day, she had to choose between attending a much-anticipated party with her friends or staying home to complete a complicated school assignment. She thought about all the advice she had gotten over time.

She asked her brother for advice, and he told her about his experiences with balancing fun and responsibilities. This helped Maya gain a new perspective on the situation.

Maya created a list of pros and cons for both options. As she weighed the advantages and disadvantages, she realized that completing her assignment would give her more long-term advantages and satisfaction.

When Maya tackled the assignment, she realized she was going to struggle if she tried to focus on the entire thing at once. She decided to break it down into smaller sections and then do it one step at a time. Each completed section made her feel more confident, and the assignment became less overwhelming.

When she experienced doubt about something, she brainstormed solutions. She experimented with different study methods, asked her teachers for guidance, and found resources online. She was proud of herself when she managed to complete her assignment ahead of time.

Her positive attitude guided her and she saw her challenges as opportunities to innovate. She also found creative ways to manage her time, such as working on her assignments before school while she juggled her studies, social life, and school work.

After she had completed her assignment, Maya took some time to reflect. She realized that although her dedication had helped her a great deal, she could still improve. She decided to work harder in the future.

Financial Mastery

Money might seem like an overwhelming subject to you, but it's entirely possible to manage it if you have the right skills. It's best to learn about budgeting and saving at a young age, as it will help you become the master of your own financial destiny.

Remember that becoming a master of your financial destiny is not about being perfect with numbers; it's just about gaining the confidence to make informed choices. When you start learning about financial management, you're gaining skills that will help you for the rest of your life. You can steer your financial ship into a future filled with adventures and opportunities.

Tips for Money Management

Let's take a look at some basic and very practical guidelines that can give you a head start when it comes to your finances. It might seem scary at first, but the sooner you start and the more you learn, the easier it will become.

Follow these tips:

- With any financial management, always start by making a budget. You need to keep track of how much money you make and how much you spend. If you know where your money's going, you'll be able to manage it better. For example, if you have a part-time job as a waitress, how much do you make a month when it comes to your salary and tips? How much money do you spend on entertainment and anything else you buy?

- When you've started to save, set a goal for yourself. If you have a clear goal, it's easier to make smart spending choices. For example, do you want to buy clothes, some new electronic gadget, or go on a trip? Another good tip when it comes to saving is that when you receive a paycheck or an allowance, put some of it into savings before you start spending the money. This can also help you build up a safety net.

- Before you're going to buy something, think about it. Is it something you really need, or do you just want it for the moment? This is also where it's necessary to prioritize between needs and wants. You should buy according to your needs and save for your wants. For example, do you want to buy shoes you actually need for sport, or is it a cute top that's over-the-top expensive that you'll only wear once or twice? Always ask yourself if you're really getting value for your money.

- This is also where we come to credit cards. They're tempting but don't use them unless you understand how they work. Debt will only cause you more stress. For example, it's tempting to rush out and buy a whole bunch of clothes or that new game that you've wanted for a long time on credit, but you're going to be paying for them for a very long time.

- Smart buying is a good way to manage your money and to make sure you don't run out of cash before the end of the month. This would involve comparing prices before you buy something. Often, you'll find the best deals when you do online shopping.

- If you can't go out on your allowance, now is the right time to step out into the world and look for a part-time job. Working part-time is not only a great way to make extra money, but can also help you get much-needed work experience. These days, it's even possible to work online. If your parents aren't keen on you out there in the dark, driving around between a job and home, it might give them peace of mind if you can find an online admin job or whatever else is available.

- Also, don't let your friends pressure you into spending a fortune. True friends will respect whatever you choose to do, whether it's to save or spend.

- Don't be afraid to ask parents, teachers, or mentors for advice on financial matters. It can also help you a great deal to learn from their experiences.

Sam's Money Journey

Sam was a savvy teenager who was known for his energy and independence. As he approached his final year in high school, he wanted to start to manage his own money. He decided to start by making a budget.

He sat down and meticulously calculated his monthly income from his part-time jobs. Then, he listed his expenses, such as clothes, entertainment, and other purchases. As he worked out the numbers, he got a clearer idea of where his money was going.

Sam decided to set goals for himself. He wanted to go on a trip with his friends after graduation and started saving toward this goal.

Sam also got creative with saving to make things easier for himself. He arranged for his paycheck to be automatically transferred to his account before he had the chance to spend the money.

He was proud of his restraint when it came to things he usually enjoyed buying, such as online games.

Sam also thought about credit cards. He was tempted, but he didn't want to fall into the debt trap. He remembered the advice he had received—that he should fully understand how credit cards worked if he wanted to use them. He didn't like the thought of having to pay off a credit card for a long time.

Sam searched for deals online and became a savvy shopper soon enough. His favorite online stores usually had better prices than the physical stores.

Sam also learned about the importance of asking for advice when he needed it. He asked his parents, teachers, and other mentors for advice. Their stories and experiences helped him find his way through the financial maze.

As graduation approached, Sam was relieved to find that the savings he had accumulated had put the road trip within his reach. He felt a sense of accomplishment.

He had managed his money wisely, embraced a growth mindset when it came to finances, and was ready to embark on his next adventure with newfound confidence.

Embrace the Journey, Not Just the Destination

Success isn't only about crossing the finish line to your goal; it's also about your journey on the way there. Think of your journey as a thrilling adventure with twists and turns that keep you on your toes. You need to immerse yourself in all the exhilarating moments of your life, even the difficult ones.

Think about all those difficult times that have helped you build resilience in life. Late-night study sessions for difficult exams, even when you feel like going to bed or going out and enjoying fun times with your friends. You're learning the ability to keep going even when times get tough. These sessions have taught you perseverance, endurance, and dedication. You know you need to keep going when you want to achieve your dreams.

All your failed attempts at something are valuable. What you think of as setbacks are stepping stones on your way to success. When something doesn't work, it's not a dead end, but an opportunity to innovate.

Your journey is also about the friends you make on the way and all the different people who have walked the path with you. It's about working together, supporting each other, and celebrating victories, even the small ones. The connections you form are actually a really valuable part of your journey.

So, make the most of the challenges that come your way. The late nights and the hard work will shape you into someone from substance, with the resilience and determination to face whatever challenges come your way. Enjoy the journey and the discoveries you make on the way.

Take Control of Your Learning

You could be the architect of your own learning and make your own discoveries. There are so many resources available these days that you can basically shape your own learning and education. A lot of free resources are available online, so there's no excuse for being uninformed. Just think of all the informative videos on YouTube. We're not talking about the celebrity or gaming ones, but the ones on topics such as history, science, politics, or psychology. Just make sure you watch and read information from reliable sources, as there are also many content creators on the internet who aren't that reliable. For example, when it comes to psychology, you might not want to watch all the videos from self-educated self-help gurus, but rather trust the content that is produced by qualified clinical psychologists. Make sure you research the person's credentials before listening to them.

Think of it as going on a treasure hunt for wisdom and that you've got the tools to sail through the sea of online videos and free courses to go on a learning adventure. The options that are available are as diverse as your interests; you can find anything from history to coding and cooking.

Ultimately, you should aim to become a lifelong learner. You want to be curious and hungry for knowledge every day of your life. When you're a lifelong learner, you'll seize every opportunity to grow and evolve.

Lifelong learning is a mindset of exploration and creativity. You enjoy learning something for the thrill of it. It's about nurturing your passions and expanding your horizons. For example, you don't have to learn just for the sake of gaining new qualifications, but you could gain practical new skills, such as cooking or baking. You could even learn some psychology just for the sake of your own self-development.

Science Tells Us Anyone Can Learn

Have you ever wondered what goes on in your brain when you're learning?

Basically, it's like a fireworks show of connections happening in your brain. When you learn something new, whether it's a grammar concept or a difficult dance move, your neurons will work together to create a special connection called a synapse. The synapse is like a bridge between your neurons that allows them to reach out to each other and share information.

The more you repeat and practice what you've learned, the stronger your synapse will become. It's almost like building a superhighway in your brain that makes it easier and faster for information to travel.

Your brain is always ready to soak up new knowledge. Neuroplasticity is your brain's ability to keep on learning and making new connections, no matter how old you are.

Neuroplasticity in Action

Imagine you want to play a tricky online game. You struggle to get past a difficult level and you repeatedly fail to kill a monster. You get frustrated and decide to try again the next day.

When you return to play again, you find your fingers are faster, your reflexes are sharper, and you're better able to dodge enemy attacks. You beat the monster quite quickly this time, and you manage to move on to the next level. So, what happened?

This is neuroplasticity in action. Your brain was still hard at work when you stepped away from the game. It was busy rewiring itself and creating new connections between neurons while strengthening the pathways responsible for your gaming skills.

Your brain adapted as you tried the difficult level repeatedly. It recognized the patterns, learned from your mistakes, and fine-tuned your movements. This is why you were better able to face the monster the next day.

Your brain is always adjusting and upgrading itself. When you're learning to draw, play a musical instrument, or learn to dance, your brain will rewire itself to get better at what you're practicing. The more you practice, the stronger your neural connections become, and you'll also get better at the skill you've been learning.

Your brain is like a super-flexible muscle. With time, effort, and practice, it can grow and improve.

Ignore the Toxic Positive Vibes

A growth mindset shouldn't be confused with constant toxic positivity. Life's not all sunshine and rainbows, and that's perfectly acceptable. Life has its difficulties, and if you're constantly ignoring your negative emotions and telling yourself that you should always look on the bright side, you're just invalidating your feelings. You'll suppress your strong emotions rather than handle them in a healthy way and process them. It's okay, not to be okay. One of the things you're going to have to learn while growing up is to deal with the difficult stuff. Your life is never going to be happy and easy all the time, but resilience will get you through the tough times. Sometimes, we just have to hold on and push through.

Think of your difficult times as having difficult days among the sunny ones. Positive vibes and telling yourself, "Don't worry, be happy," is just not going to work all the time. If you try to fake a smile when you actually feel awful, you'll just end up pushing your challenging emotions away in an unhealthy way.

If you're on a growth mindset and lifelong learning journey, you have to embrace all your emotions and all the ups and downs. You need to give yourself permission to feel whatever you're feeling, even if it's frustration, confusion, or sadness.

Activity: Navigating Authentic Feelings

We all experience a range of emotions, and it's important to acknowledge them without brushing them aside. Let's take a closer look at some common toxic positivity phrases and then look at some healthier alternatives. It's okay to feel your feelings.

Toxic positive phrases

- Just think positive and everything will be fine.
- Good vibes only!
- Don't worry, be happy.
- It could always be worse.
- Look on the bright side.
- Negative thoughts bring negative outcomes.

Healthier alternatives

- It's okay to feel a mix of emotions. What can I learn from this situation?
- It's alright to have ups and downs. How can this challenge help me to grow as a person?
- I'm allowed to acknowledge my worries and feelings. How can I support myself?
- It's healthy to acknowledge both the positive and negative aspects of something. How can I find balance in my perspective?
- Addressing my concerns doesn't mean I'm inviting negativity. How can I deal with difficulties in a positive way?

This activity encourages you to shift from brushing aside your feelings to embracing them and finding healthier ways to cope. Finding healthy and positive ways to deal with your emotions is an important part of personal growth.

Turning Your Inner Critic Into a Helpful Guide

We've all had those times when our inner critic made us doubt ourselves and our abilities. You're not power-less when it comes to your negative thoughts. This step-by-step guide helps you turn your negative thoughts into more positive and realistic ones. So, embrace your unique journey and create a positive mindset that's ready to conquer the world.

How to Turn Your Negative Thoughts Into Positive Ones

- One idea to deal with that negative voice in your head is to give it a name—calling it "Doubtful Danny" or "Sad Sally" will help you separate yourself from these thoughts and to see yourself as being separate from them. It's almost like giving your inner critic its own personality. That's one way of showing the negative thoughts that you're in charge of them.
- Take notice of the stories your inner critic loves to tell you. Does it tell you that you just aren't good enough and things will never work out for you? Instead of a thrilling adventure, the stories your mind tells you are mostly based on doubts

and worries. Your own "Doubtful Dylan" might tell you that things will never go your way, but remember, you're the director of your own story, and you can rewrite the script in any way you want. It's up to you to see how you can rewrite your story.

- It's time to take control and rewrite your own story. Try to rewrite your story with a more balanced perspective. So, stand up to your inner voice when it tells you that you can't do something. Failure is just a step on your road to success.

- Your inner critic is trying to protect you in most situations, even though it's not doing so in the healthiest way. So, you should thank it and let it know that you've got things handled.

- Take things one step at a time. Break complicated things down into smaller, manageable tasks. If you feel like you're going to get overwhelmed by negative thoughts, just focus on the next step. When the negative little voice in your mind tells you that you can't do something, tell them that you can, one small step at a time. Each victory will make you feel more confident.

For example, imagine you have to do your first-ever speech at your school assembly. You're feeling nervous and you're doubting yourself. You take a deep breath and remember your mother's advice to take things one step at a time. Then only do you focus on the next step, namely, to step onto the stage. As you step onto the podium, you tell yourself you can do this. With every word you speak, your confidence grows as you conquer your fear.

- Our thoughts can also get carried away and tell us things for which there is no evidence. When you have a doubtful thought about yourself, ask yourself if there is evidence of this and if things really are as bad as you think they are. For example, you may think you're bad at social interaction if you've embarrassed yourself in front of someone. However, you should look back at your past social interactions and ask yourself if things are really that bad. You've attended parties and made new friends during different times of your life, so you can't really be as bad as you think you are. You should also challenge your negative thoughts by creating alternative explanations for your situation and by just learning from it as much as you can and moving forward. Maybe things didn't happen perfectly, but there might be a different perspective, and it doesn't mean you failed.

We've all felt, at times, like we've failed at socializing. Don't let these negative thoughts get you down. Take a step back and think about all the times you've actually had successful social interactions—the laughs at parties, the new friends you've made. Maybe you've had awkward times, but you don't have to let it define you. Try looking at it from another angle—maybe that awkward moment is just a small moment in the larger picture. You've learned, you've grown, and your inner negative voice is getting quieter. So, keep on forward with the wisdom you've gained.

- Celebrate that you're unique and that there's no one quite like you. Don't compare yourself to others, especially not to those on social media. Focus on your own growth. Your path in life is just as valuable as somebody else's.

WHEN YOU GET KNOCKED DOWN, IT'S TIME TO GET UP AGAIN!

Maybe you've heard the acronym "Bounce Back." It's an acronym for some of the most important principles of resilience.

B—Bad times won't carry on. Things will get better in your life.

O—Others can only help you if you share with them.

U—Unhelpful ways of thinking will only make you feel worse.

N—Nobody is perfect. We're all human and we all make mistakes.

C—Concentrate on the good things you have in your life, even if they seem small.

E—Everyone suffers and experiences setbacks. This is just a normal part of life.

B—Blame fairly. You'll find that negative things are often caused by a combination of things you did, things others did, and maybe you just had bad luck.

A—Accept things you can't change and change what you can.

C—Catastrophizing will only make things worse.

K—Keep things in perspective. Even a bad moment will only be one moment of your life.

Billy Bounces Back

Billy usually had a confident and happy outlook on life, but he struggled with some of his school subjects that he needed to gain admission into a prestigious university. He failed two of his subjects and started thinking that he just wasn't smart enough to achieve his goals.

Days turned into weeks, and Billy found himself lost in a sea of self-doubt. He couldn't shake the thought that he might not achieve his goals, that his dreams were slipping away. His usual laughter was replaced by quiet contemplation, and his confidence slowly disappeared.

His older sister saw he was having some trouble and asked him what was bothering him.

Billy hesitated before opening up about his failures and the cloud of doubt that had settled over him. His sister listened patiently and then told him something that changed his journey.

She told him that everyone has to face setbacks and it was how you bounce back from it that mattered. She said it was no different from the challenges he had to overcome before.

His sister also told him that intelligence wasn't about knowing everything immediately, but that it was about perseverance, hard work, and a willingness to learn from mistakes.

Inspired by his sister, Billy decided he wouldn't let failure define him. He would bounce back, as he had so many times in the past. He asked his teachers for extra help, attended study groups, and dedicated his time to understanding the subjects that seemed impossibly difficult to him.

Billy began to see progress after some months of hard work. Difficult concepts began to make sense to him, and his confidence increased. He realized that intelligence was a journey and not a destination.

When Billy had to retake the exams, he faced the test with a newfound sense of purpose, armed with the knowledge that he had worked hard to understand the material. And when the results were announced, he had not only passed but achieved high grades in both subjects.

Billy gained a renewed sense of self-belief. He had faced his challenges head-on and bounced back stronger than ever.

Boosting Your Resilience

You can boost your resilience by doing all kinds of fun activities. Sometimes, it's just about boosting your positive self-talk:

- Write yourself a letter of encouragement, almost as if you're talking to your best friend. When you have to deal with setbacks, read the letter to remind yourself of your strengths.

- You can do a story swap, but for this one, you will need some willing "victims." Get your friends together, and share some stories of challenges you've faced and how you overcame them.
- Try to find some resilient role models. You can research stories of people who managed to overcome challenges and hardships. Their journeys should inspire you to keep pushing yourself. These could even be people in your life, like parents, teachers, or even grandparents. It's even better if they're people you know, and you can talk to them in person.
- You've probably heard this before, but keeping a growth journal really works. Write about some setbacks you faced and the lessons you learned. How did these experiences make you stronger?
- Tackle a resilience challenge with your friends. This could be anything from a hike to a creative project or even a school assignment. Dealing with challenges as a team will strengthen your bond and resilience.
- Make a safe haven of encouragement for yourself by creating a positive wall for yourself.

You could decorate a wall in your bedroom with sticky notes of quotes and positive affirmations that remind you of your strength.

THE 7 CS OF RESILIENCE

Life is full of unexpected challenges. The 7 Cs of Resilience is a powerful tool that can help you get through them. Each "C" refers to a key aspect of building resilience, the skill that helps you bounce back from setbacks and adversity.

1. Challenges

Life's challenges are like puzzles waiting to be solved. Embrace them as opportunities to learn and grow. After all, every challenge you conquer is a step closer to becoming the amazing person you're meant to be. For example, if you're struggling with one of your subjects at school, don't just give up on it. Keep on studying and trying, even if you think your grades aren't good enough. Get a tutor to help you manage your challenges if you're able to do so.

2. Control

Choose to focus on what you can control. There are things you can change and things you can't. Instead of worrying about the uncontrollable, channel your energy into making positive choices. For example, maybe you're not that great at sports, but you can focus on getting as fit as you can and enjoying yourself.

3. Connection

Surround yourself with supportive friends, family, and mentors. Reach out when you need a helping hand or a listening ear. Remember, your support network is there to catch you when you fall. For example, if you have a specific problem or challenge in your life, share it with people you can trust. It's not good for your mental health to keep your struggles to yourself.

4. Competence

You're capable of more than you think. Recognize your strengths and skills. Every time you conquer a challenge, you'll become more competent. Believe in yourself and your ability to tackle whatever comes your way. It can take a while to build competence, for example, if you're learning something new, like a language. Be patient with yourself and give yourself time to build competence.

5. Coping

Life's twists and turns can be tough, but if you've got good coping skills, it's much easier to manage. The trick is to find healthy ways to manage your stress and keep your mind clear. This can include journaling, practicing mindfulness, and doing regular exercise. For example, journaling regularly, even if it's only for a few minutes a day, can help you clear your mind.

6. Confidence

Believe in yourself and your potential. Remind yourself of your past successes and the hurdles you've overcome. People with self-confidence use it as a shield to protect them against self-doubt, and it keeps them moving forward. Confidence also helps you get back up and move on after a setback. For example, if you fail an exam, don't think of yourself as a failure and that you'll never succeed.

7. Calm

Take a break when you feel overwhelmed. Practice self-care, like listening to your favorite music, going for a walk, or simply taking a moment to breathe. Calmness helps you regain control and face challenges with a clear mind.

Lily's Story

Lily found herself facing a challenge that left her feeling increasingly anxious. She had always struggled with public speaking, and now her history teacher had announced a class presentation that would count for a significant portion of her grade.

Lily remembered hearing about the 7 Cs of Resilience —a tool to help navigate life's challenges. She decided to try them in the hope that they would help her feel more confident for the presentation.

Lily saw the presentation as a challenge and an opportunity to learn and grow. Instead of letting fear control her, she embraced it as a chance to conquer her fear.

She knew she couldn't control everything, but she focused on what she could control—her preparation and effort. She practiced her speech, researched her topic, and visualized herself succeeding.

Feeling overwhelmed, Lily connected with her friends and family for support. They offered her encouragement and support.

With each practice session, Lily recognized her increasing competence. She acknowledged she had strengths that involved being able to do thorough research and she could also explain concepts clearly.

As the presentation day approached, Lily faced moments of stress. She turned to healthy coping mechanisms, like taking short breaks to walk outside and practicing deep breathing to calm her nerves. She also made sure to drink enough water, as she always got a dry mouth when she got anxious.

On the day of the presentation, Lily was nervous but also determined when she faced her classmates. She reminded herself of past successes and setbacks she had overcome. Even if the presentation wasn't perfect, she had the confidence to face it head-on.

During her presentation, Lily took a deep breath and managed to stay calm. She focused on her words and found her rhythm. She felt accomplished after she finished her presentation.

INTERVIEW ACTIVITY—DISCOVERING GRIT AND RESILIENCE

Connecting with someone who has demonstrated perseverance and grit to achieve their goals can teach you a thing or two about resilience. As you know, resilience is that special ability that helps people overcome challenges and setbacks with determination and strength. When you speak with someone who embodies this mindset, you can gain valuable insight into their strategies, journey, and mindset.

Perseverance interview worksheet

Your name:

————————————————————————————

Person's name (interviewee):

————————————————————————————

Date of interview:

————————————————————————————

Keep the following interview etiquette in mind:

- Ask for permission to do the interview, even if it's someone you know.
- Choose a time that will suit the person you want to interview and that will also work for you.
- Practice your questions beforehand. When you do the interview, you want to come across as someone who knows what you're doing.
- Be polite and respectful during the interview. Listen carefully to what the other person has to say.
- Ask the person for permission to contact them again if you should need to do so.

Suggested questions:

- Can you tell me more about a significant goal you set for yourself and that you managed to achieve?
- What steps did you take to accomplish that goal?
- Where did you find your inspiration to pursue this goal?
- How did you overcome challenges or obstacles?
- Did you ever feel like giving up? If so, how did you manage to stay motivated?
- How did achieving this goal impact your life? Or how has your life changed after achieving it?

Reflection on interview

Think carefully about what you've learned from the person after the interview. How does the person's journey relate to resilience and overcoming challenges? Create some kind of feedback project about your interview. You could write it down or create a visual presentation.

We're almost at the end of our journey and our final chapter will look at how you can use your newfound confidence and skills to go out there and build the life you deserve. After all, good things happen to those who work for them, not those who sit around waiting for something to happen.

OWN IT: T—TAKE INITIATIVE

L et's dive into the world of self-care, goal setting, and accountability—the keys to unlocking your full potential and achieving everything you've ever dreamed of. Now is the time to learn how to take charge of your life, both physically and mentally. You can become the architect of your own future if you set goals and take accountability for your actions.

SELF-CARE PART 1: YOUR PHYSICAL NEEDS

You're all ready to set your goals and start working on achieving your dreams in life. However, first of all, you must look after yourself, both physically and mentally. Sleep, food, and exercise... that's the name of the game.

Nourishing Your Body

Your physical well-being will keep you going on your journey through life. We get it; you're not rookies when it comes to knowing about sleep, food, and exercise. Don't worry; we're not going to talk about the same old story. Just keep in mind that taking care of yourself isn't just a "should;" it's a "must" if you want to achieve your dreams.

About your diet—don't worry; we're not about to drop a "no fast food, no energy drinks" bomb on you. Those occasional indulgences are part of living and enjoying life. However, there needs to be balance. You also need to understand what exactly you're putting into your body. Knowledge is power and can help you make better decisions.

Water? Hydration? This may sound boring, but the truth is, your brain needs water. It needs water like a car needs fuel—to keep your body running smoothly.

Your brain is your main ally in your adventure of life, so you need to feed it the best brain foods. Superfoods like nuts, seeds, and berries will keep your brain working at its best capacity.

Nuts

Nuts are like treasure chests of the essential vitamins and minerals that your brain needs to function optimally. They're packed with healthy fats that will keep your brain running.

For example, walnuts contain lots of omega-3 fatty acids. They're brain boosters that fight bad guys like inflammation and help your thinking and memory improve.

Keep in mind that nuts also contain a lot of fat, so you shouldn't go crazy and eat an entire bag in one sitting. It's all about balance, so stick to about ¼ cup a day. You can have them as snacks, put them in your salad, or even mix them with your veggies. They're also fantastic as part of a granola or trail mix. You can create yourself an energy-boosting snack that's better than anything you'll find in the store.

Leafy Greens

Okay, we know leafy greens don't sound exciting, but they're actually like a magical booster potion for your brain.

Your greens like kale and spinach are full of vitamin E, carotenoids, and flavonoids. These are fancy, big words, but they have a really important function. They protect your brain from memory loss and foggy thinking. They also contain folate, which makes sure your red blood cells are working well and can kick your brain's neurotransmitters into action. The neurotransmitters help your brain send signals and stay sharp.

Fermented Foods

Fermented foods are made by mixing regular foods with microorganisms like yeast and bacteria. They create tasty and gut-friendly treats like yogurt and sauerkraut. You can think of them as the rebels of the kitchen that add excitement to your plate.

This exciting lineup can consist of plain yogurt with active cultures, kimchi, sauerkraut and kombucha. They bring in the bacteria that let your gut work and run smoothly like a well-oiled machine. If you have a happy gut, you'll experience less anxiety and be happier overall.

Avocados

Avocados are your brain's buddy because they're full of magnesium, a special nutrient that can boost your brain's productivity and your mood. When your brain is running low on magnesium, you may start to feel down in the dumps. Avocados are great on their own or as part of a salad or sandwich.

Dark Chocolate

If you've always thought chocolate was an unhealthy snack, you weren't entirely correct. Dark chocolate can bring joy to your taste buds and your brain. It's packed with iron, which is like armor for your neurons, and can even boost your mood. Dark chocolate with not too much sugar is best for your brain.

Sleep—Your Circadian Cycle

Your circadian rhythm is almost like the conductor of an orchestra, which helps your body's functions work together in harmony. It directs your energy, alertness, and mood, but as the sun sets, your circadian rhythm slows down, and your body feels the need to rest.

Your circadian rhythm can be disturbed by different things. For example, it can be thrown off if you decide to binge-watch Netflix until dawn. When your circadian rhythm doesn't align with your natural light-dark cycle, you'll find a shift in your sleep-wake cycle.

During your teenage years, your sleep-wake cycle could take you on a wild ride. Suddenly, you're a night owl who stays up way past your usual bedtime because you simply can't fall asleep if you go to bed earlier. There's actually a scientific reason behind this, and it's all about your body clock.

Your body's circadian rhythm gets a type of makeover during your teenage years. It could start producing the sleep hormone melatonin later at night and then takes time again to wind down in the morning. This is partly to blame on your pesky hormones that cause growth spurts and other exciting changes in your body.

On the positive side, this late-night energy surge could make you feel productive and creative late at night. However, the early school cycle might not work for your night owl tendencies and leave you yawning through your morning classes.

Sleep Tips

A messed-up sleep cycle can be extremely annoying. Just imagine—some nights you lay wide awake, and you can't manage to shut off your brain until the early hours of the morning, while on other nights you're cold as soon as you switch your lights off. Sleep interrupters like having to study for an exam, a busy social life, sneaky social media notifications, or Netflix binges could all play a role when it comes to keeping you up. However, we've got some tips that can help you get a better night's sleep.

Try these tips to fix your circadian rhythm:

- You should stick to a sleep schedule to keep your circadian rhythm consistent. Our bodies love predictability and you can train your brain when to produce more energy or dim the lights.
- Create a comfortable sleep sanctuary. Your bedroom should be dark, cool and quiet. If it's too light and loud, you'll just lay awake for hours.
- Banish the use of screens in your bedroom. Around an hour before bedtime, your eyes need a break, as the blue light will just mess up your sleep routine.
- Don't have a heavy meal, like that juicy steak, just before bedtime. If your stomach is too full, you just won't be able to snooze.
- Move your body throughout the day, and make sure you get enough exercise, but not too shortly before bedtime. Exercise close to bedtime can also mess up your circadian rhythm.
- Maybe caffeine is not for you, but if you enjoy your coffee, you should avoid having it in the afternoon and evening. It's like a circadian rhythm and energy boost.
- If you want your brain to switch off, you need to wind down. Read a book, take a warm bath, or practice mindfulness.

Exercise

Your life is probably a whirlwind of activity. It's classes, homework, sports, friends, parties, and then sometimes for a social media scroll. The idea of doing 30 minutes of exercise a day might sound crazy but it's actually completely doable.

Managing your time to fit in exercise may seem like a challenge, but if you only use a few minutes of your 24 hours a day to exercise, it can make a world of difference to your day, and it can give you the energy to focus on everything else on your to-do list.

More exercise can also help you sleep better. The trick is not to make it into another chore but to do fun things, like dancing to your favorite tunes, going for a jog with friends, or playing a fun sport.

When exercise is part of your daily routine, you're boosting your physical health, and you're fueling your mind. When you boost your mood, it also becomes easier to achieve success.

If you exercise daily, you can also use the time to bond with family and friends.

Benefits

Exercise can help you become the superhero that you're meant to be.

Regular exercise has the following benefits:

- Exercise will help your body and its functions run smoothly. It gives your blood a turbo boost and will help it reach every corner of your body.
- Are you worried about extra weight? Don't let social media give you weight hangups. However, exercise can help you to keep your weight in check.
- Exercise is also good for your heart and can help keep your cholesterol levels healthy and keep your blood pressure in check.
- You'll also find it easier to release your stress, and you'll feel lighter than air.
- Exercise can also give you a glow and boost your self-confidence to new levels.
- Exercise is also good for your bones and prevents them from getting weak and wobbly.

SELF-CARE PART 2: EMOTIONAL NEEDS

We've talked about physical care, but guess what? There's a whole universe of self-care beyond that—emotional, mental, spiritual, environmental, recreational, and social. We're going to take a look at the emotional and spiritual side of things.

Have you ever wondered why things make you feel a certain way? Emotions can show what's going on inside you.

Pay attention to your feelings. Whether it's joy, anger, or that mix of butterflies before a big moment, knowing what makes you feel certain things is like having a secret power to navigate your life.

Your Spiritual Self-Care

Spiritual self-care is not only for those of us who follow a specific religion. It's also about connecting to your inner soul and keeping it healthy.

To be able to practice spiritual self-care, you need to understand what it actually is.

It's about connecting to the universe or whatever higher power you believe in. If you struggle to believe in this, it's perfectly fine, too. You could look at spiritual self-care as caring for yourself on a deeper level. You have to listen to your intuition to be able to take care of yourself on a spiritual level.

When you're able to develop a strong intuition, you'll know what your soul needs to be happy and healthy.

We may lack this intuition about what we need on a spiritual level, as our ability to tune into our spiritual needs is often clouded by the hectic lives we lead.

However, you can do the following to get in touch with your spiritual side:

- It's worth your while to give meditation a try. Meditation can help you strengthen your focus and find calm. There are different apps and videos that can put you on the right road when it comes to meditation.
- Mindfulness can help you to be present in the moment and to feel connected to yourself, those around you, and your surroundings.
- Spending time in nature, such as going for hikes, swimming at the beach, or even just sitting outside under a tree, can put you in touch with your spiritual self and the universe.
- You can also learn about spirituality by exploring different beliefs. You don't have to commit to a specific religion or belief, but exploring the different perspectives can help you find what works for you.
- Sometimes, sitting quietly and really listening to your thoughts can also help you get more in touch with your spiritual side.
- Volunteering and helping others could also be a spiritual experience. Making a positive contribution to life, in general, can help you feel more connected to the world around you.

Environmental Self-Care

Your environment can also affect how you feel and there are things you can do to make it as positive as possible.

You've probably had your mom nagging at you to clean up after yourself and to keep your room organized. "Boring!" may have been the first word in your mind, but your mom is actually right. A clutter-free space can help you feel calmer and think more clearly. You'll also be more productive if you can find your stuff quickly.

Plants can purify the air and bring some fresh vibes into your bedroom or study space. Not only do they look awesome, they're also little parts of nature.

You can also freshen up your space by letting in some natural light. Open your curtains to let the natural light in during the daytime. It will lift your mood.

Add more positivity and personality to your room by giving it your personal touch. Think of the empty walls in your room as a blank canvas, and change it any way you like by using your thoughts and ideas. Use colors, textures, and any object that means something to you.

Once you've set up your room the way you want it, you should create a chill spot where you can relax, listen to music, or read. This can be the perfect place to go when you need a break.

Different scents and aromas can also boost your mood. A diffuser can fill your space with the calming scent of essential oils.

Also, remember to show the planet some love by recycling. Do all those eco-friendly things, such as recycling your plastic bottles.

Recreational and Social Self-Care

Make sure you also have time for recreational and social self-care. Life can be hectic, but you need to set time aside for hobbies and activities you enjoy.

Whatever you enjoy doing, it will remind you of what makes your life awesome. Hanging out with your friends can also give your soul all the positivity you need. Plan some fun, like going to the movies, or just have some fun chill sessions where you can share stories, laugh, and vent.

While you probably enjoy spending time with your friends, make some time for yourself as well. Do some things alone, like walking, reading, or writing, as this will also help you recharge.

Do a digital detox from time to time; take that social media break and make time for real-life interactions.

Step away from the screen, enjoy the present moment, and have a face-to-face chat with someone.

Make sure to form connections in your community. Join some volunteer groups, sports teams, and clubs. You can also make fantastic new friendships when you connect with others who share your passions.

Celebrate your friends and stay supportive of each other. Listen, encourage each other, and be there for your friends during tough times.

PLANNING TO REACH THOSE BIG DREAMS

Everyone needs goals in life, including you. Goals give you direction and something toward which to work. They can help you stay focused on positive activities. Goals can also challenge you to step out of your comfort zone and develop new skills. This can encourage your personal growth and help you build confidence.

Working toward a goal can also help you deal with challenges and focus on building resilience, which means it will be easier for you to bounce back from setbacks and keep going.

Locke and Latham's Goal Setting

The grandpas of goal-setting wisdom, Locke and Latham, first published their goal-setting theories in 1968. They encourage setting measurable and challenging goals.

Let's take a look at their principles for goal setting:

- Your goals should be as clear as a neon sign in the night. Everyone should be able to get them immediately.
- Set challenging goals, but you should also be able to achieve them. Your goals shouldn't be easy, but also not completely out of your reach. They need to be doable and in your control.
- Your heart should be in achieving your goals, and you need to be committed to putting in the work.
- Welcome feedback you receive because you need to know how you're doing. You need to be able to change your strategy if things aren't going great.

Well, why not set some goals of your own?

GOAL SETTING WORKSHEET

Answer these questions as honestly as possible:

Choose your dream: What's that big, exciting thing you want to achieve?

Write it down here:

_____

Break down your dream into smaller, specific goals. For example, if you want to be a writer, you first need to make sure that your grammar and spelling are up to scratch.

Goal 1: _____
Goal 2: _____
Goal 3: _____

Make sure your goals are challenging but achievable.

Decide when you want to reach your goals. Be realistic but don't give yourself forever.

Deadline for goal 1: _____
Deadline for goal 2: _____
Deadline for goal 3: _____

How will you tackle each goal? Break it into small steps.

Steps for goal 1: _____

Steps for goal 2: _____

Steps for goal 3: _____

Who can support you on your journey? Share your goals with them!

Supportive person 1: _____

Supportive person 2: _____

Supportive person 3: _____

Create mini-goals within your goals. This can help you track your progress and make changes where needed.

Checkpoint for goal 1: _____

Checkpoint for goal 2: _____

Checkpoint for goal 3: _____

Write a positive affirmation that'll keep you going, even when things get tough. For example, "I've got the power to achieve my dreams!"

My positive affirmation: _____

Plan a reward for yourself when you reach your goals. It could be a movie night, a treat, or a day out with friends.

Reward for goal 1: _____

Reward for goal 2: _____

Reward for goal 3: _____

DOING WHAT IT TAKES TO SUCCEED

There are certain things you can do to get closer to success. So, let's dive in with some energy and inspiration to help you reach your goals.

One of the first things you need to do is to say farewell to any idealistic ideas of perfection you have. Aim high, but don't get stuck in fixing the small details. Make mistakes, learn, and grow.

Stop putting things off. Procrastination is tempting, but you'll never reach your destination if you get too caught up in the details.

Passion is truly the one thing that can keep you going in life. Love what you're doing, and it will never feel like work. Find something to fill up your days that makes your heart race and your energy levels soar.

Remember that your mindset will always be important in whatever you decide to do. Positivity, resilience, and self-esteem will keep you going when setbacks are threatening to hold you back.

How do you supercharge your confidence while you're busy conquering your dreams? Well, now that you've set your goals, you have to achieve them! Confidence is ultimately about believing in yourself, trusting your abilities, and facing your challenges head-on.

Once you've set your goals, you know where you are going and how to get there. This sense of purpose will help you stay confident and focused.

Pay It Forward by Letting Others Know the Power of OWNing It

I hope that this book has made you feel understood and that it has eliminated many of the doubts and challenges that may have been stopping you from being your best self. You now know why self-esteem, self-confidence, and the other vital "selfies" take a little work. You also know that a specific set of strategies makes it much easier to make friends, stand up for yourself, and be the captain of your own emotions.

The teen years are a time of incredible change, but you can rise to every challenge by applying the skills detailed in the OWN IT method.

I hope you can share a bit about the impact this book has had on your own life so other teens know where to go for the practical guidance they need.

IN UNDER 1 MINUTE
YOU CAN HELP OTHERS JUST LIKE YOU BY LEAVING A REVIEW!

I know how busy your days can be! Homework, extracurricular activities, friends, family—sometimes it seems like they are all competing for your attention.

It will take just a few seconds to let others know that this book can help them harness their own inner strength to emerge as confident, resilient, empowered teens. Please help me spread the word.

Scan the QR code below

CONCLUSION

We've come to the end of our journey, and it's time to take a look at what we've learned.

First of all, we've used the OWN IT method to navigate our personal growth journey:

- **Owning your path:** You've embraced your own path and have accepted yourself for the unique person you are. You're ready to make your authentic way through the world, not just follow the crowd. You don't fall prey to strange social media trends and influences.
- **Working through challenges:** You're going to conquer setbacks and bounce back. Failing one exam won't cause you to give up on your schoolwork.

- **Navigating tech and social media:** You've decided you will learn how to use technology to your advantage, but not let it rule your life. You care about what you watch or read on social media and aim to consume positive and healthy content.
- **Investing in your well-being:** You invest in your mental and physical health, and build a solid foundation for the future.
- **Taking smart risks:** You're stepping out of your comfort zone and chasing your dreams.

Your journey doesn't have to start with dramatic changes. You can do it one step at a time, every day, and the pieces will gradually fall into place. Decide who you want to be, and start steering your life in this direction.

It's about making choices that feel right for you and not living your life according to what others would expect. However, cultivating a strong and independent mindset also means you'll be able to make a positive contribution to society.

This book can be your key to unlocking the world you want to create for yourself. By the time you finish reading, you'll have the right tools that will put you on that next level when it comes to managing your life and making it great.

BE MOTIVATED!

We hope we have guided you through practical advice and engaging activities to become motivated and empowered as you discover your path in life.

The different chapters provided you with the following useful information:

- In Chapter 1, we introduced the ideas that lay the groundwork for personal growth: self-esteem, self-confidence, self-love, and self-respect. We highlighted how these concepts can help you create a strong sense of self, which is essential when it comes to forming healthy relationships with others.
- In Chapter 2, we explored the intricate connection between your body and mind. We demystified the teenage brain and offered you some insight into the changes that shape your thoughts and emotions. The chapter also addressed stress and gave you the tools to manage it.
- Chapter 3 told you to own your worth and how you need to take ownership of your life. We shared strategies to protect yourself from negativity and bullies, as well as giving you tips on how to respect and love yourself.

- Chapter 4 equipped you with the tools to recognize, express, and manage your emotions. We also taught you a thing or two about making connections and setting healthy boundaries.
- Chapter 5 provided a lifeline for those who battle fear and anxiety. You were shown how to overcome your fears step by step by following the gradual exposure technique.
- Mindset shifts in Chapter 6 looked at the power of our minds. By cultivating a growth mindset and honing your decision-making skills, you can learn from your challenges and become resilient.
- Chapter 7 looked at taking initiative, also when it comes to looking at yourself, emotionally and physically.

We look forward to receiving feedback about your experiences so that you can inspire others who are on a similar path. Please leave a review on Amazon to tell us how this book has improved your life for the better. Let's uplift each other and create a community that thrives on positivity and growth.

ABOUT THE AUTHOR

Dr. Emma Sky holds a Ph.D. in integrative medicine and has dedicated over two decades of her life to spearheading mindfulness practices and transformative group therapies. With a focus on self-healing and personal growth, she has diligently served with a non-profit organization, empowering individuals to improve and promote their well-being.

Emma believes that healing the body begins with healing the mind and a holistic approach to health.

She is passionate about helping teens get the most out of these amazing years and helping them get on the path to the best start to adult life.

REFERENCES

British Heart Foundation. (2018, May 14). *Active listening*. British Heart Foundation. https://www.bhf.org.uk/informationsupport/heart-matters-magazine/wellbeing/how-to-talk-about-health-problems/active-listening

Carroll, D. W. (n.d.). *The relationship between thoughts, feelings and behaviors – Debbie Woodall Carroll*, LPCC-S. https://debbiewoodallcarroll.com/the-relationship-between-thoughts-feelings-and-behaviors/

Cherry, K. (2021, February 1). *Why toxic positivity can be so harmful*. Verywell Mind. https://www.verywellmind.com/what-is-toxic-positivity-5093958

Cleveland Clinic. (2022, January 11). *Vagus nerve: Gastroparesis, vagus nerve stimulation & syncope*. Cleveland Clinic. https://my.cleveland clinic.org/health/body/22279-vagus-nerve

Cooks-Campbell, A. (2022, May 26). *What self-love truly means and ways to cultivate it*. Www.betterup.com. https://www.betterup.com/blog/self-love

Cotoia, A. (2020, May 10). *Limbic system - the definitive guide*. Biology Dictionary. https://biologydictionary.net/limbic-system/

Crestani, J. (2023, July 6). *Building self-confidence through setting and achieving goals*. Medium. https://medium.com/lampshade-of-illumination/building-self-confidence-through-setting-and-achieving-goals-9da330b9cf12

Crevin, M. (2020, July 14). *Listen more, talk less and other tips for better communication*. Your Teen Magazine. https://yourteenmag.com/family-life/communication/ways-to-improve-communication

Dhaliwal, R. (2018, January 30). *How does the teenage brain work?* White Swan Foundation. https://www.whiteswanfoundation.org/life-stages/adolescence/the-working-and-development-of-the-teenage-brain

Drury, J. (2017, October 6). *Why it's important to have self-respect in life and at work.* HRM Online. https://www.hrmonline.com.au/section/strategic-hr/important-self-respect-life-work/

Esther. (2020, March 25). *10 spiritual self care ideas for a healthy soul.* Through the Phases. https://www.throughthephases.com/spiritual-self-care-ideas/

Family Lives. (2022, October). *How does bullying affect your child? | Family Lives.* Www.familylives.org.uk. https://www.familylives.org.uk/advice/bullying/advice-for-parents/how-does-bullying-affect-your-child

Far, S. (2016, June 2). *20 questions to ask yourself when you feel fear.* Inc.com. https://www.inc.com/samira-far/20-questions-to-ask-yourself-when-you-feel-fear.html

Felton, A. (2022, September 1). *Limbic system: What to know.* WebMD. https://www.webmd.com/brain/limbic-system-what-to-know

Gemma Brown Coaching. (2022, April 4). *Journaling for well-being: Identify your values.* Gemma Brown Coaching. https://www.gemmabrowncoaching.co.uk/post/journaling-for-well-being-identify-your-values

Ginsburg, K. (2019, May 29). *Building resilience: The 7 Cs.* Center for Parent and Teen Communication. https://parentandteen.com/building-resilience-in-teens/

Good Therapy. (2018, May 26). *Confidence Pick-Me-Up! Self-Esteem Quotes to Boost Your Mood.* https://www.goodtherapy.org/blog/confidence-pick-me-up-self-esteem-quotes-to-boost-your-mood-0526187

Health Encyclopedia. (2019). *Exercise and teenagers - health encyclopedia.* University of Rochester Medical Center. Rochester.edu. https://www.urmc.rochester.edu/encyclopedia/content.aspx?ContentTypeID=90&ContentID=P01602

Jeanette, L (2023, March 8). *21 important self-acceptance activities - Teaching Expertise.* Www.teachingexpertise.com. https://www.teachingexpertise.com/classroom-ideas/acceptance-activity/

LauraJane Illustrators. (2023, March 31). *5 actionable steps to help you reframe negative self-talk.* Laura Jane Illustrations. https://laurajaneil

lustrations.com/blogs/blog/5-actionable-steps-to-help-you-reframe-negative-self-talk

Lawson, K. (2009). *What are thoughts & emotions? | Taking charge of your health & wellbeing.* Taking Charge of Your Health & Wellbeing. https://www.takingcharge.csh.umn.edu/what-are-thoughts-emotions

Lindsay. (2016, May 11). *7 habits of highly effective teens-be proactive.* Triumph Youth Services. https://triumphyouthservices.com/7-habits-of-highly-effective-teens-be-proactive/

Narikaa. (n.d.). *Dealing with the opposite sex.* Narikaa.com.https://narikaa.com/article/adolescence/adolescent-sexuality/dealing-with-the-opposite-sex/

Pietrangelo, A. (2020, March 29). *The effects of stress on your body.* Healthline. https://www.healthline.com/health/stress/effects-on-body

Robledo, I. (2022, January 15). *Self esteem journal prompts for teens.* Making Mindfulness Fun. https://www.makingmindfulnessfun.com/self-esteem-journal-prompts-teens/

Ross, A. (n.d.). *Do today's teens have it harder or easier than past generations?* The Swarm. https://novatoswarm.org/1629//do-todays-teens-have-it-harder-or-easier-than-past-generations/

Tompkins, M. A., PhD, & ABPP. (n.d.). *Six tips to help your teen procrastinate less. cognitive therapy in the San Francisco Bay area.* https://www.sfbacct.com/teen-topics/six-tips-to-help-teen-procrastinate-less

UCLA Health. (n.d.). *Sleep and teens - sleep disorders | UCLA Health.* Www.uclahealth.org. https://www.uclahealth.org/medical-services/sleep-disorders/patient-resources/patient-education/sleep-and-teens

VanDuzer, T. (2020, October 23). *Time management techniques for teens: The ultimate guide.* Student-Tutor Education Blog. https://student-tutor.com/blog/time-management-techniques-for-teens/#google_vignette

Yolanda. (2022, August 3). *30 self love journal prompts to boost self esteem.* Put the Kettle On. https://putthekettleon.ca/self-love-journal-prompts-boost-self-esteem/

Youaremom. (2019, May 8). *Self-awareness and self-acceptance in adolescence*. You Are Mom. https://youaremom.com/children/self-acceptance-in-adolescence/

Your Therapy Source. (2022, August 11). *SMART goals for teens*. Your Therapy Source. https://www.yourtherapysource.com/blog1/2022/08/11/smart-goals-for-teens-3/

Youth Empowerment. (2019, November 6). *Challenging negative self-talk*. Youth Empowerment. https://youthempowerment.com/challenging-negative-self-talk/

Printed in Great Britain
by Amazon